HOMO SAPIENS PART - V

HUMANITY UNVEILED: A POETIC JOURNEY THROUGH FOURTEEN REFLECTIONS

MAWPHNIANG NAPOLEON

Made with ♥ on the Notion Press Platform
www.notionpress.com

To my dear readers, with hearts so true,

This book of verse is yours alone to keep.

Your interest and support, I do renew,

And thank you for the time you took to peep.

I hope this book has brought you joy and cheer,

And that the words within have touched your soul.

For writing is my passion, dear and dear,

And I hope to bring you more stories to roll.

With each new verse and every rhyme,

I strive to bring you pleasure and delight.

So please, do keep on reading, line by line,

For in your hearts, my words will take their flight.

With gratitude, I thank you all once more,

For reading and supporting me, so sure.

Contents

Foreword

It is with great honor that we introduce to you, "Homo Sapiens Part V: Humanity Unveiled: A Poetic Journey through Fourteen Reflections" written by Mawphniang Napoleon. This fifth book in the series of "Homo Sapiens" explores the complex and ever-evolving human experience through the lens of poetry.

In "Eco-Balance: A Call to Action," Napoleon delves into the importance of preserving our planet and the urgent need for action. "The Dichotomy of Technology: Balancing Progress and Preservation" explores the delicate balance between advancing technology and preserving our natural world.

"The Wandering Mind: A Poem on the State of Absentmindedness" takes us on a journey through the state of mind that often leads us away from the present moment. "The Quest for Reality: A Journey Through the Depths of Understanding" explores the human desire to understand the world and our place in it.

"The Cosmic Tapestry: Striving for Unity and Understanding in a World of Ethnic Divides" delves into the complexities of understanding and unifying different cultures. "The Quest for Meaning: A Poem on Religion" delves into the human need for spiritual connection and understanding.

"The Placebo Paradox: A Tale of Healing and Challenges" explores the power of the mind in healing and the challenges that come with it. "Etched in Stone: Reflections on Life, Death, and Legacy" reflects on the impact of our actions on the world and the legacy we leave behind.

"Eternal Embrace: A Poem on the True Nature of Love" delves into the complexities and beauty of love. "Eternal Radiance: A Poem on the Many Forms of Beauty" explores the different forms of beauty that exist in the world.

Finally, "The Pursuit of Knowledge: A Lifelong Journey of Understanding and Empowerment" explores the lifelong pursuit of knowledge and the ways in which it empowers us.

We hope that you will enjoy reading this book as much as we have enjoyed bringing it to you. Mawphniang Napoleon's poetry will take you on a journey through the human experience, leaving you with a deeper understanding and appreciation of the world around you.

Preface

It is an honor for us to introduce you to "Homo Sapiens Part V: Humanity Unveiled: A Poetic Journey through Fourteen Reflections." This book is the fifth in the series of books "Homo Sapiens" written by Mawphniang Napoleon. In this book, the author explores the themes of Eco-Balance: A Call to Action, The Dichotomy of Technology: Balancing Progress and Preservation, The Wandering Mind: A Poem on the State of Absentmindedness, The Quest for Reality: A Journey Through the Depths of Understanding, The Cosmic Tapestry: Striving for Unity and Understanding in a World of Ethnic Divides, The Quest for Meaning: A Poem on Religion, The Placebo Paradox: A Tale of Healing and Challenges, Etched in Stone: Reflections on Life, Death, and Legacy, Eternal Embrace: A Poem on the True Nature of Love, Eternal Radiance: A Poem on the Many Forms of Beauty, and The Pursuit of Knowledge: A Lifelong Journey of Understanding and Empowerment.

The author's unique and thought-provoking perspective on these topics is sure to leave readers with a deeper understanding of the world around them. We believe that "Homo Sapiens Part V" is a must-read for anyone interested in exploring the complexities of human existence through the lens of poetry.

We are grateful to Mawphniang Napoleon for sharing his insights and talents with us and are confident that "Homo Sapiens Part V" will be a valuable addition to any reader's library. We hope that you will enjoy reading this book as much as we did and that it will inspire you to continue your own journey of understanding and empowerment.

Thank you for taking the time to read this book and for your interest in the "Homo Sapiens" series. We look forward to sharing more of Mawphniang Napoleon's work with you in the future.

Acknowledgements

We would like to extend our deepest gratitude to all of the people who have helped us throughout the journey of creating this book. From our family and friends who have supported us, to the mentors who have guided us and the peers who have inspired us, we are truly grateful for all of the ebbs and flows of our lives that have helped shape us into the individuals we are today. Your unwavering support and encouragement have been invaluable in bringing this book to fruition. We would also like to thank the readers who have taken the time to engage with our work and for your interest in our book. We look forward to continuing to grow and evolve as writers and individuals, and we hope that our book will be a reflection of that journey.

We would also like to thank our editor for their invaluable contributions, providing insightful feedback and helping us shape the final product. We are grateful for the time and effort put in by our designer for creating the beautiful cover and layout of the book. Our publicist has done an amazing job in promoting our book and we are extremely grateful for their hard work. We would also like to thank the librarians, booksellers, and bloggers who have helped spread the word about our book and have helped make it accessible to readers. We are truly grateful for the support of our literary community.

Last but not least, we would like to express our appreciation for our publisher for believing in our work and for providing us with the opportunity to share our story with the world. We are humbled and honored to have our book published under their banner.

Thank you all for your support and we hope that you enjoy reading our book as much as we enjoyed writing it.

A Team

Prologue

Welcome, dear readers, to the fifth installment in the series of books "Homo Sapiens" written by Mawphniang Napoleon. We are honored to present to you "Homo Sapiens Part V: Humanity Unveiled: A Poetic Journey through Fourteen Reflections." This book delves into the complex and ever-evolving world of humanity, exploring themes of eco-balance, the dichotomy of technology, the wandering mind, the quest for reality, the cosmic tapestry, religion, healing, legacy, love, beauty, and knowledge.

Through poetry and reflection, we embark on a journey through the depths of understanding and strive for unity and understanding in a world of ethnic divides. We explore the paradox of healing, the eternal embrace of love, and the pursuit of knowledge as a lifelong journey of empowerment.

This book is a call to action for us to reflect on our actions and their impact on the world around us. It is a reminder of our responsibility to preserve and protect our planet for future generations. It is an invitation to dive deep into the human experience and discover the beauty, wonder, and complexity that lies within each and every one of us.

We hope that this book will leave a lasting impression on you, inspiring you to reflect on your own journey and to strive for a greater understanding of the world and humanity. So, without further ado, let us begin our poetic journey through "Homo Sapiens Part V: Humanity Unveiled."

1. Eco-Balance: A Call to Action

As the dawn breaks and the sun arises,

A new day begins with fresh surprises.

But as we gaze upon the world so fair,

A dire reality is brought to bear.

The forests wilt, the oceans rise,

The creatures of the earth are met with demise.

Man's insatiable greed and reckless plight,

Has led to ecological destruction in full sight.

The depletion of natural resources,

And the pollution of our sources,

Has brought about a catastrophic end,

To the delicate balance that nature intended.

The depletion of natural resources,

And the pollution of our sources,

Has brought about a catastrophic end,

To the delicate balance that nature intended.

But it is not too late to make amends,

To heal the wounds and mend the trends.

Through conservation and sustainable living,

We can ensure the earth's continued thriving.

So let us take responsibility,

For our actions and their gravity,

And work towards a brighter future,

Where ecological destruction is no longer a suture.

But alas, the task is not without its hurdles,

For many are the obstacles and hurdles,

That stand in the way of progress,

And impede the path towards egress.

The apathy of the masses,

And the stubbornness of the classes,

Who profit from the destruction of our land,

Stand in opposition to the call of conservation's hand.

But we must not falter in our quest,

For the survival of our earth is at its best,

We must rise up and make our voices heard,

For the sake of all that is good and just, not absurd.

For the future of our planet, we must fight,

With all our strength and all our might,

For the sake of our children and the generations to come,

We must protect and preserve, not destroy and succumb.

So let us not be idle in our ways,

But instead, let us pave the path towards better days,

For the fate of our earth and all its inhabitants,

Is in our hands, and it is time to take our stance.

The earth is our home, and it's up to us to preserve,

To take care of it, and to conserve.

The future of our planet depends on our actions,

And the impact that we make in each and every transaction.

We must understand the consequences of our deeds,

And the impact that they have on the earth and all its seeds.

We are all connected in this vast, intricate web,

And we must all play our part, not just one or a few, but all ebb.

We must learn to live in harmony with nature,

And to respect and appreciate its grandeur.

We must learn to tread lightly on this earth,

And to give back more than we take, in equal worth.

The time for change is now, not tomorrow,

For every day that passes, we borrow,

From the earth's resources and its future,

And it's up to us to take action and make a suture.

Let us not be remembered as the generation that destroyed,

But as the one that stood up, and employed

All of its efforts towards the preservation,

Of this beautiful earth, our only true possession.

As we journey on this path of right,

We must not forget to keep in sight,

The importance of empathy and compassion,

For all living creatures, in every situation.

For the earth is not just our abode,

But a home for millions of creatures and nodes,

Each with their own unique purpose and role,

In the grand scheme of nature's whole.

We must learn to share this earth with all,

And to heed the call of nature's call.

For in the end, it is not just about us,

But about the balance and harmony of all.

Thus, let us take a stand against ecological destruction,

And work towards a brighter, more sustainable solution.

Let us strive for a future where nature and man coexist,

And our actions reflect our love and respect for this earth that we exist.

For the earth is our legacy and our responsibility,

And it's up to us to ensure its continuity,

For the sake of all that is good and just,

Let us work towards ecological preservation, a must.

So let us not be blinded by our own short-sightedness,

But open our eyes to the world's vastness.

Let us not be swayed by the allure of immediate gain,

But consider the long-term impact of our actions, in refrain.

For the earth is a delicate balance,

Of intricate systems and cycles that enhance,

The beauty and wonder of this world,

And it's up to us to ensure that it unfurled.

We must learn to live in harmony with nature,

And to recognize our role as a creature.

We must learn to take only what we need,

And to sow the seeds of conservation with speed.

For the earth is not just a resource to be exploited,

But a treasure to be cherished, respected and avoided,

From the smallest microbe to the tallest tree,

All life on earth is interconnected, and we must see.

So let us take a stand against ecological destruction,

And work towards a brighter, more sustainable solution,

For the sake of this earth, our home and our legacy,

Let us strive for ecological preservation, a true rarity.

We must understand that our actions have consequences,

And that our choices will shape the earth's defenses.

We must take responsibility for our impact on the land,

And make a concerted effort to heal, not to damage or to brand.

We must learn to live in balance and in peace,

With the earth, its creatures and its ecosystems,

We must learn to be stewards of this world,

And to leave it better than we found it, not unfurled.

We must learn to think beyond ourselves,

And to consider the impact of our actions on all else,

For the earth and its creatures are not just for us to use,

But to coexist with, in a state of mutual benefit, not abuse.

We must learn to value the earth not just for its resources,

But for its beauty, its wonder, and its forces.

We must learn to protect and preserve,

Not just for ourselves, but for all and for ever.

And let us not forget the power of education,

For it holds the key to true conservation.

We must teach the next generation,

The importance of sustainability and preservation.

We must instill in them, a love for the earth,

And the importance of protecting its worth.

We must give them the tools and the knowledge,

To make informed decisions and take action to acknowledge.

For it is the youth who will shape the future,

And it is their actions that will nurture.

We must guide them and provide them with the means,

To be the change that the world needs, to lean

Towards a sustainable future for all,

Where the earth's resources are not exploited and fall,

Where the balance of nature is not disrupted,

And where the cycle of life is not corrupted.

So let us take a stand against ecological destruction,

And work towards a brighter, more sustainable solution.

Let us strive for a future where nature and man coexist,

And our actions reflect our love and respect for this earth that we exist.

2. The Dichotomy of Technology: Balancing Progress and Preservation

In the age of technology, where screens and wires rule supreme,

We see a world of advancements, a never-ending dream.

But as we march forward, with machines at our command,

Do we truly understand the consequences at hand?

The proliferation of technology, an exponential growth,

Has brought us convenience and power, an unending flow.

But as we become more reliant on machines to sustain,

Do we lose sight of what it means to be human? The question remains.

The dichotomy of technology, both boon and bane,

Is a conundrum that requires deep contemplation and refrain.

For as we harness its power, to improve our lives and fate,

We must also consider its impact on our humanity's state.

The ethics of technology, a complex and nuanced field,

Requires us to ponder the implications and yield.

For as we create artificial intelligence, and machines that can think,

We must consider their autonomy and potential to shrink

The human experience, reducing us to mere machines.

Thus, we must tread carefully, in this age of machines.

For as we continue to push the boundaries of what is possible,

We must also consider the impact on our souls and principal.

Technology, a double-edged sword,

Brings us great advancements, yet also great discord.

Thus, as we continue to march forward, with machines at our side,

We must remember to consider the human experience and abide.

by striking a balance, between progress and preservation,

Between innovation and contemplation, with careful deliberation.

For as we strive to improve our lives, with technology's aid,

We must not forget the importance of being human, and the value of our humanity's grade.

It is a delicate dance, between man and machine,

A balancing act that requires careful routine.

For as we continue to harness technology's power,

We must also consider its impact on humanity's future hour.

For technology is not just a tool, a means to an end,

But a reflection of ourselves, and the values we defend.

And as we continue to shape the world with technology's might,

We must remember to uphold our humanity, and guide it to the light.

Thus, let us embrace technology, with open and thoughtful minds,

And use it to improve our lives, while also being kind.

For as we continue to march forward, in this age of machines,

We must remember to keep our humanity at the forefront of our schemes.

As we delve deeper into the realm of technology,

We must not forget the importance of empathy.

For as we create machines that can think and feel,

We must also consider their rights and what is real.

The question of sentience, a contentious one,

Requires us to ponder the implications of what's begun.

For as we create artificial intelligence, with increasing capability,

We must also consider their moral responsibility.

The question of consciousness, a philosophical debate,

Requires us to ponder the nature of self and fate.

For as we create machines that can think and feel,

We must also consider the nature of their being and appeal.

The implications of technology, a vast and varied field,

Requires us to ponder the future and what's concealed.

For as we continue to push the boundaries of what is possible,

We must also consider the impact on our planet and its sustainable cycle.

As we delve further into the realm of technology,

We must not forget the importance of humanity's dignity.

For as we create machines that can think and feel,

We must also consider the impact on human life, and what is real.

The question of autonomy, a crucial one,

Requires us to ponder the implications of what's begun.

For as we create artificial intelligence, with increasing capability,

We must also consider the right to self-determination and ability.

The question of ethics, a complex one,

Requires us to ponder the impact of our actions on the future and what's begun.

For as we create machines that can think and feel,

We must also consider the moral and ethical implications and appeal.

The implications of technology, a vast and varied field,

Requires us to ponder the future and what's concealed.

For as we continue to push the boundaries of what is possible,

We must also consider the impact on our society and its sustainable principles.

As we continue to advance, with technology's aid,

We must remember to consider the consequences, and the price we have paid.

For as we create machines that can think and feel,

We must also consider the impact on humanity's dignity, and what is real.

Technology, a powerful force,

Brings us great advancements, yet also great remorse.

Thus, as we continue to march forward, with machines at our side,

We must remember to consider the implications, and to be guided by what is right, and dignified.

As we delve deeper into the realm of technology,

We must not forget the importance of accountability.

For as we create machines that can think and feel,

We must also consider who is responsible for their actions, and what is real.

The question of accountability, a crucial one,

Requires us to ponder the implications of what's begun.

For as we create artificial intelligence, with increasing capability,

We must also consider who is liable for their actions, and ability.

The question of ownership, a complex one,

Requires us to ponder the impact of our actions on the future and what's begun.

For as we create machines that can think and feel,

We must also consider the legal and ethical implications of ownership and appeal.

The implications of technology, a vast and varied field,

Requires us to ponder the future and what's concealed.

For as we continue to push the boundaries of what is possible,

We must also consider the impact on our society and its legal principles.

Technology, a powerful force,

Brings us great advancements, yet also great remorse.

Thus, as we continue to march forward, with machines at our side,

We must remember to consider the implications, and to be guided by what is right, dignified, and accountable.

As we delve further into the realm of technology,

We must not forget the importance of diversity.

For as we create machines that can think and feel,

We must also consider the impact on different cultures and what is real.

The question of diversity, a crucial one,

Requires us to ponder the implications of what's begun.

For as we create artificial intelligence, with increasing capability,

We must also consider the representation and inclusivity of different cultures and ability.

The question of bias, a complex one,

Requires us to ponder the impact of our actions on the future and what's begun.

For as we create machines that can think and feel,

We must also consider the ethical implications of bias and appeal.

The implications of technology, a vast and varied field,

Requires us to ponder the future and what's concealed.

For as we continue to push the boundaries of what is possible,

We must also consider the impact on our society and its cultural principles.

Technology, a powerful force,

Brings us great advancements, yet also great remorse.

Thus, as we continue to march forward, with machines at our side,

We must remember to consider the implications, and to be guided by what is right, dignified, accountable and diverse.

As we delve deeper into the realm of technology,

We must not forget the importance of privacy.

For as we create machines that can think and feel,

We must also consider the impact on personal data and what is real.

The question of privacy, a crucial one,

Requires us to ponder the implications of what's begun.

For as we create artificial intelligence, with increasing capability,

We must also consider the protection and security of personal data and ability.

The question of surveillance, a complex one,

Requires us to ponder the impact of our actions on the future and what's begun.

For as we create machines that can think and feel,

We must also consider the ethical implications of surveillance and appeal.

The implications of technology, a vast and varied field,

Requires us to ponder the future and what's concealed.

For as we continue to push the boundaries of what is possible,

We must also consider the impact on our society and its privacy principles.

As we delve deeper into the realm of technology,

We must not forget the importance of sustainability.

For as we create machines that can think and feel,

We must also consider the impact on the environment and what is real.

The question of sustainability, a crucial one,

Requires us to ponder the implications of what's begun.

For as we create artificial intelligence, with increasing capability,

We must also consider the ecological impact and ability to conserve resources and ability.

The question of waste, a complex one,

Requires us to ponder the impact of our actions on the future and what's begun.

For as we create machines that can think and feel,

We must also consider the ethical implications of waste and appeal.

As we delve deeper into the realm of technology,

We must not forget the importance of security.

For as we create machines that can think and feel,

We must also consider the impact on the safety and what is real.

The question of security, a crucial one,

Requires us to ponder the implications of what's begun.

For as we create artificial intelligence, with increasing capability,

We must also consider the protection of information and ability to secure from cyber-attacks and ability.

The question of cybercrime, a complex one,

Requires us to ponder the impact of our actions on the future and what's begun.

For as we create machines that can think and feel,

We must also consider the ethical implications of cybercrime and appeal.

As we delve deeper into the realm of technology,

We must not forget the importance of creativity.

For as we create machines that can think and feel,

We must also consider the impact on human creativity and what is real.

The question of creativity, a crucial one,

Requires us to ponder the implications of what's begun.

For as we create artificial intelligence, with increasing capability,

We must also consider the possibility of replacing human creativity and ability.

The question of originality, a complex one,

Requires us to ponder the impact of our actions on the future and what's begun.

For as we create machines that can think and feel,

We must also consider the ethical implications of originality and appeal.

The implications of technology, a vast and varied field,

Requires us to ponder the future and what's concealed.

For as we continue to push the boundaries of what is possible,

We must also consider the impact on our society and its creative principles.

As we continue to advance, with technology's aid,

We must remember to consider the consequences, and the price we have paid.

For as we create machines that can think and feel,

We must also consider the impact on creativity and originality, and what is real.

In conclusion, technology, a powerful force,

Brings us great advancements, yet also great remorse.

Thus, as we continue to march forward, with machines at our side,

We must remember to consider the implications, and to be guided by what is right, dignified, accountable, diverse, private, sustainable, secure, and creative.

As we delve deeper into the realm of technology,

We must not forget the importance of human connection.

For as we create machines that can think and feel,

We must also consider the impact on human interaction and what is real.

The question of connection, a crucial one,

Requires us to ponder the implications of what's begun.

For as we create artificial intelligence, with increasing capability,

We must also consider the possibility of replacing human connection and ability.

The question of socialization, a complex one,
Requires us to ponder the impact of our actions on the future and what's begun.
For as we create machines that can think and feel,
We must also consider the ethical implications of socialization and appeal.
The implications of technology, a vast and varied field,
Requires us to ponder the future and what's concealed.
For as we continue to push the boundaries of what is possible,
We must also consider the impact on our society and its connection principles.
As we continue to advance, with technology's aid,
We must remember to consider the consequences, and the price we have paid.
For as we create machines that can think and feel,
We must also consider the impact on human connection and socialization, and what is real.
As we delve deeper into the realm of technology,
We must not forget the importance of human autonomy.
For as we create machines that can think and feel,
We must also consider the impact on human decision-making and what is real.
The question of autonomy, a crucial one,
Requires us to ponder the implications of what's begun.
For as we create artificial intelligence, with increasing capability,
We must also consider the possibility of replacing human autonomy and ability.
The question of agency, a complex one,
Requires us to ponder the impact of our actions on the future and what's begun.
For as we create machines that can think and feel,
We must also consider the ethical implications of agency and appeal.
The implications of technology, a vast and varied field,
Requires us to ponder the future and what's concealed.
For as we continue to push the boundaries of what is possible,

We must also consider the impact on our society and its autonomy principles.

As we continue to advance, with technology's aid,

We must remember to consider the consequences, and the price we have paid.

For as we create machines that can think and feel,

We must also consider the impact on human autonomy and agency, and what is real.

As we delve deeper into the realm of technology,

We must not forget the importance of human autonomy.

For as we create machines that can think and feel,

We must also consider the impact on human decision-making and what is real.

The question of autonomy, a crucial one,

Requires us to ponder the implications of what's begun.

For as we create artificial intelligence, with increasing capability,

We must also consider the possibility of replacing human autonomy and ability.

The question of agency, a complex one,

Requires us to ponder the impact of our actions on the future and what's begun.

For as we create machines that can think and feel,

We must also consider the ethical implications of agency and appeal.

The implications of technology, a vast and varied field,

Requires us to ponder the future and what's concealed.

For as we continue to push the boundaries of what is possible,

We must also consider the impact on our society and its autonomy principles.

As we continue to advance, with technology's aid,

We must remember to consider the consequences, and the price we have paid.

For as we create machines that can think and feel,

We must also consider the impact on human autonomy and agency, and what is real.

Technology, a powerful force,

Brings us great advancements, yet also great remorse.

Thus, as we continue to march forward, with machines at our side,
We must remember to consider the implications, and to be guided by what is right, dignified, accountable, diverse, private, sustainable, secure, creative, connected, and autonomous.

3. The Wandering Mind: A Poem on the State of Absentmindedness

Oh state of absentmindedness, so oft maligned,

But in thy depths, doth wisdom oft reside.

For in thy grasp, the mind doth wander free,

Unshackled from the mundanity of life.

Thou art the realm of the introspective,

Where the self doth delve into its core.

And in thy depths, the soul doth find,

The answers to life's eternal lore.

But oft thy grasp doth lead to confusion,

And thoughts doth spiral into chaos.

Thus, thy state must be wielded with care,

For in thy depths, doth madness also pause.

But in thy absence, the mind doth stagnate,

Trapped in the mundanity of daily toil.

Thus, a balance must be struck between,

The state of absentmindedness and toil.

For in the ebb and flow of thy presence,

Lies the key to understanding all.

And in thy grasp, the mind doth transcend,

To a state of enlightenment, standing tall.

So let us not malign thy state,

But embrace thy depths with open arms.

For in thy grasp, doth true wisdom lie,

And in thy absence, doth true ignorance charm.

And in thy grasp, the mind doth soar,
To realms beyond this mortal coil.
Where the mysteries of existence,
Are revealed in a kaleidoscope of toil.
But in thy grasp, there lies a danger,
The mind may get lost in thy embrace.
And so, one must tread with caution,
And find the balance in this race.
For in thy absence, the mind is dull,
And in thy presence, it may stray.
Thus, one must find the middle ground,
And find the balance in this fray.
And in this balance, one will find,
The answers to life's eternal quest.
For in the state of absentmindedness,
Lies the key to true inner rest.
So let us embrace thy state with grace,
And find the balance in thy depths.
For in thy grasp, doth true wisdom lie,
And in thy absence, doth true ignorance bequeath.
And in this wandering, we shall find,
The answers to life's eternal quest.
For in the state of absentmindedness,
Lies the key to true inner rest.
But let us not forget the cost,
Of losing oneself in thy embrace.
For in thy depths, one may find,
That the self is lost in an endless race.
Thus, one must tread with care,
And navigate thy depths with skill.
For in thy grasp, doth true wisdom lie,

But also the potential to be ill.
And so, let us find the balance,
Between the state of absentmindedness and the mind.
For in this balance, true enlightenment,
Is the ultimate reward we shall find.
For in thy grasp, the mind doth transcend,
To a state of pure and utter bliss.
And in thy absence, the mind doth suffer,
Trapped in a world of mundanity and miss.
Oh state of absentmindedness, so oft maligned,
But in thy depths, doth wisdom oft reside.
For in thy grasp, the mind doth wander free,
Unshackled from the mundanity of life.
And in this wandering, we shall find,
The answers to life's eternal quest.
For in the state of absentmindedness,
Lies the key to true inner rest.
So let us embrace thy state with grace,
And find the balance in thy depths.
For in thy grasp, doth true wisdom lie,
And in thy absence, doth true ignorance bequeath.
But let us not forget that wisdom,
Is not always found in thy embrace.
For in thy absence, the mind doth focus,
And in that focus, true purpose takes place.
For in the state of absentmindedness,
We may lose sight of our goals.
And in our wandering, we may find,
That we've lost control of our souls.
Thus, we must find the balance,
Between the state of absentmindedness and the mind.

For in this balance, true enlightenment,

Is the ultimate goal we shall find.

And in this balance, we shall see,

That the state of absentmindedness is not all bad.

For in its grasp, we find true freedom,

And in its absence, true purpose is had.

So let us not malign thy state,

But embrace thy depths with open hearts.

For in thy grasp, doth true wisdom lie,

And in thy absence, true purpose starts.

So let us embrace thy state with grace,

And find the balance in thy depths.

For in thy grasp, doth true wisdom lie,

And in thy absence, true purpose bequeaths.

But let us not forget that wisdom,

Is not the only thing we gain.

For in the state of absentmindedness,

We find creative ideas, free from chain.

In thy depths, the mind doth flow,

With new and fresh perspectives.

And in thy grasp, we find inspiration,

That will be the key of our own adventures.

Thus, we must find the balance,

Between the state of absentmindedness and the mind.

For in this balance, true enlightenment,

Is the ultimate goal we shall find.

And in this balance, we shall see,

That the state of absentmindedness is not all bad.

For in its grasp, we find true freedom,

And in its absence, true purpose is had.

So let us embrace thy state with grace,

And find the balance in thy depths.

For in thy grasp, doth true wisdom lie,

And in thy absence, true purpose bequeaths.

So let us not fear the state of absentmindedness,

But embrace it with open hearts.

For in its grasp, we find true freedom,

And in its absence, true purpose starts.

But let us not forget that freedom,

Is not without its own cost.

For in the state of absentmindedness,

We may lose sight of what matters most.

In thy depths, the mind doth roam,

And in its wanderings, may forget.

The obligations and responsibilities,

That make our lives worth living yet.

Thus, we must find the balance,

Between the state of absentmindedness and the mind.

For in this balance, true enlightenment,

Is the ultimate goal we shall find.

So let us not fear the state of absentmindedness,

But embrace it with open hearts.

For in its grasp, we find true freedom,

And in its absence, true purpose starts.

But let us not forget our obligations,

And find the balance that we need,

For in the state of absentmindedness,

Lies the key to true inner peace.

And in this balance, we shall see,

That the state of absentmindedness is not just a curse.

For in its grasp, we find true freedom,

And in its absence, true purpose and purpose.

So let us embrace thy state with grace,

And find the balance in thy depths.

For in thy grasp, doth true wisdom lie,

And in thy absence, true purpose bequeaths.

The state of absentmindedness,

A double-edged sword it may be.

But in its balance, true enlightenment,

Is the ultimate destiny.

And in this enlightenment, we shall see,

That the state of absentmindedness is not to be feared.

For in its grasp, we find true freedom,

And in its absence, true clarity is cleared.

So let us not malign thy state,

But embrace thy depths with open hearts.

For in thy grasp, doth true wisdom lie,

And in thy absence, true purpose starts.

So let us not fear the state of absentmindedness,

But embrace it with open hearts.

For in its grasp, we find true freedom,

And in its absence, true purpose starts.

But let us not forget our obligations,

And find the balance that we need,

For in the state of absentmindedness,

Lies the key to true inner peace.

And in this peace, we shall find,

The true meaning of our existence.

For in the state of absentmindedness,

Lies the key to true coexistence.

So let us embrace thy state with grace,

And find the balance in thy depths.

For in thy grasp, doth true wisdom lie,

And in thy absence, true purpose bequeaths.
And in this balance, we shall find,
The true meaning of our being.
For in the state of absentmindedness,
Lies the key to true understanding.
So let us not malign thy state,
But embrace thy depths with open hearts.
For in thy grasp, doth true wisdom lie,
And in thy absence, true purpose starts.
Oh state of absentmindedness, so oft maligned,
But in thy depths, doth wisdom oft reside.
For in thy grasp, the mind doth wander free,
Unshackled from the mundanity of life.

4. The Quest for Reality: A Journey Through the Depths of Understanding

Oh reality, thy nature doth perplex

For what is real, and what is but a text?

A mere construct, of our limited mind

Or something more, of a cosmic kind?

Perception doth shape our understanding

Yet, the world remains ever expanding

What we know, a mere drop in the sea

Of all that is, and all that may be

Is reality but a grand illusion

A phantom, fleeting in its fusion

Or is it solid, immutable

A truth, unyielding, irrefutable

Perhaps, it is a balance, a scale

Of perception and truth, never stale

For as we evolve, so does the truth

And what was once real, becomes uncouth

So let us ponder, and let us seek

For the essence of reality, unique

For in its discovery, we may find

A new perspective, for our limited mind.

But what of the subjective realm,

Where emotions and thoughts overwhelm?

Is it separate from objective truth

Or just another aspect of reality's proof?

The answer may lie in the unity
Of the subjective and objective, a community
For as our inner world influences our outer view
It is clear, they are not separate, but one and true
But what of the ultimate reality,
The one that lies beyond our ability
To fathom with our mortal mind,
Is it something we will ever find?
Perhaps it is a mystery, forever bound
A secret, that will never be found
But one thing is certain, in our quest
Reality is not something to be possessed
It is a journey, ever-evolving
A path, that is constantly revolving
So let us embrace the unknown,
For in reality, there is much to be shown.
This is not a final truth
but a journey of discovery, of youth
As we move forward, let us not forget
The beauty and complexity of reality, as yet.
But as we journey on this path of reality,
let us not forget the humility
of our own existence, in the grand scheme
of things, we are but a mere dream
For in the vast expanse of time and space
our worries and concerns seem out of place
Yet still we strive to understand
the intricacies of our own land
We search for meaning, for purpose,
in the face of the universe's endless surface
But perhaps, the search itself is enough,

to give our existence, a sense of significance, tough
For in the end, what is reality
but a manifestation of our own ability
to perceive, to comprehend,
to give shape to the world, until the very end
So let us embrace the mystery,
and let our curiosity be the key
to unlock the secrets of reality,
and in that, find serenity.
But, as we unravel the complexity
of reality, let us not forget the fragility
of our own existence and the impact
we have on the world, in fact
For as we seek to understand
the nature of reality, it's in our hands
to shape the world we live in,
and the impact it will have on the future and kin
Our actions, thoughts, and beliefs
shape the reality we perceive
So let us be mindful, let us be kind
for in reality, we are all intertwined
And as we continue on our quest
let us not forget to do our best
to make the world a better place
for all, with love and grace
For in the end, it's not just about
unlocking the secrets, but living it out
Reality is not just a matter of the mind
but a matter of the heart, of all mankind.
And thus, we come to the end of our journey,
through the labyrinth of reality, with a sense of wonder and a sense of urgency

For in this quest to understand the world around us,

we must not only expand our knowledge but also our compassion and trust.

For in reality, there is more than meets the eye

There are layers of complexity and depth that defy

Our limited understanding and yet, it is our duty

To strive for a deeper comprehension, with humility and beauty

For reality is not just a concept, it's a living entity

That constantly evolves and shapes our destiny

So let us embrace the unknown, and let us be open

To the possibilities that reality has yet to reveal, unbroken.

For in this quest for understanding, we may find

that the true reality is not just what's confined

within our minds, but what lies within our hearts,

where true knowledge and wisdom truly starts.

And as we strive to comprehend,

the depths of reality, let us not pretend

that we have all the answers, for it is a never-ending quest

A journey, that will always be ongoing, and always be the best

For reality is not a destination, but a path

that we must tread, with every step, with every breath

And as we walk this path, let us not forget

that we are but a small part of the greater whole, and yet

Our actions, thoughts, and beliefs

can shape the reality we perceive

So let us be conscious, let us be wise

For in reality, we all have a role to realize

For it is not just about understanding

But about living and co-creating

A world that is just, and true,

And in that, finding the meaning and purpose of reality, anew.

Thus, our epic journey through the realm of reality comes to an end,

But the quest for understanding and wisdom never shall end.

5. The Cosmic Tapestry: Striving for Unity and Understanding in a World of Ethnic Divides

In ancient days of yore, when man first walked the earth,

He knew not of the labels that would later give him worth.

No notion of the tribe or nation, no concept of the race,

No understanding of the boundaries that would later mark his place.

But as the years progressed, and man began to thrive,

He started to divide himself, to separate and divide.

He built walls and borders, and defined them with a name,

And thus was born the notion of the ethnic, the one of fame.

But what is ethnic, truly, if not a man-made construct,

A way to classify and judge, a way to do neglect?

For every label given, there's a group left out,

And thus the cycle of oppression, is what it's all about.

So let us question, this notion of the ethnic,

And strive for unity, for the cosmic.

For in the grand scheme of things, we're all but mere mortals,

And our ethnicities, mere mortal portals.

Let us break down the barriers, that keep us apart,

And come together as one, with a united heart.

For in the end, we're all but stardust,

And our ethnicities, mere illusions, that we must.

So let us strive for harmony, and not for separation,

For in the end, that is the true revelation.

Let us embrace our diversity, with open arms,

And create a world, where ethnic harms.

will be no more.
But as we strive for unity, let us not forget,
The rich tapestry of culture, that makes us unique, and yet
A part of something greater, a cosmic symphony,
A diverse choir, singing in harmony.
Let us celebrate our differences, and learn from one another,
For in diversity lies strength, like the leaves of a clover.
Each leaf unique, yet together, a symbol of unity,
A reminder that despite our differences, we're all one entity.
But as we journey towards a world of unity,
We must also acknowledge, the harsh reality
Of those who seek to oppress, and maintain their power,
By using ethnic divides, to divide and cower.
Let us not be swayed by their rhetoric of hate,
But instead, let love and compassion, be our fate.
For in the end, our ethnicities, should not define us,
But rather, our actions and character, should shine and astound us.
So let us strive for unity, and let it be our quest,
To build a world, where ethnic divides, are put to rest.
For in the grand scheme of things, we're all but mere mortals,
But together, we can create a world, that is truly, truly immortal.
But as we strive for unity, let us not forget,
The rich history and heritage, that make us unique, and yet
A part of something greater, a cosmic symphony,
A diverse choir, singing in harmony.
Our ethnicities are like the colors of a painting,
Each one adding depth and meaning, to the final stunning
Masterpiece, that is humanity, a work of art,
A reflection of the beauty, of a cosmic heart.
But as we admire the painting, let us not forget,
The struggles and the pain, that make it truly set

A part of something greater, the story of our past,

And the journey that we've taken, to make this painting last.

For our ethnicities are not just labels, they are stories,

Of our ancestors and their struggles, their joys and their glories.

And as we honor and respect, these stories of the past,

We pave the way for a future, where unity will truly last.

So let us strive for unity, and let it be our quest,

To build a world, where ethnic divides, are put to rest.

For in the grand scheme of things, we're all but mere mortals,

But together, we can create a world, that is truly, truly immortal.

But unity is not just about erasing our differences,

It's about embracing them, and making them our strengths.

For in our diversity lies the beauty of humanity,

A reflection of the cosmic diversity and its infinity.

Let us not see our ethnicities as a source of division,

But as a source of enrichment, and a path to true fusion.

A fusion of ideas, cultures, and traditions,

A fusion that will bring us closer, to true resolution.

For the resolution of our humanity, lies in understanding,

That we are all connected, and our differences are just branding.

A branding that sets us apart, but also brings us together,

A branding that makes us unique, but also makes us better.

So let us strive for unity, and let it be our quest,

To build a world, where ethnic divides, are put to rest.

For in the grand scheme of things, we're all but mere mortals,

But together, we can create a world, that is truly, truly immortal.

Let us celebrate our diversity, and let it be our anthem,

For in diversity we find strength, and true understanding.

A world where we are all equals, and our ethnicities, just a part,

Of the rich tapestry of humanity, woven together, heart to heart.

But unity is not just about words and good intentions,

It's about taking action, and standing against oppression.

For the divide that ethnicities create, is often used,

To justify discrimination, and to abuse.

We must stand up against racism, and bigotry,

And fight for equality, for all humanity.

We must challenge the systems, that keep us apart,

And work towards a world, where ethnic harmony is the art.

We must educate ourselves, and others too,

On the rich diversity, that makes us all anew.

We must listen and learn, from different cultures and traditions,

And strive to build a world, where everyone's voice is heard in unison.

We must challenge the narrative, that pits us against each other,

And work towards a world, where love and respect are our true brothers.

We must strive for unity, and let it be our guide,

For in unity, we find strength, and a future where ethnic divides, are no more inside.

But true unity cannot be achieved, without addressing,

The injustices of the past, and the ongoing oppression.

For too long, certain ethnic groups, have been marginalized,

Their voices silenced, and their rights privatized.

We must acknowledge, the privilege and power,

That some ethnicities have, while others cower.

We must work towards, true reparations,

For the harm that has been caused, by past generations.

We must challenge the status quo, and strive for true equity,

For a world where everyone has the same opportunity.

We must work towards, a world where everyone can thrive,

Where everyone's voice is heard, and everyone is alive.

But this is not an easy task, and the journey will be long,

But if we come together, we can make it strong.

We must strive for unity, and let it be our guide,

For in unity, we will find the strength, to create a world, where ethnic divides,

are no more inside.

So let us strive for unity, and let it be our quest,

To build a world, where ethnic divides, are put to rest.

For in the grand scheme of things, we're all but mere mortals,

But together, we can create a world, that is truly, truly immortal.

But let us not forget, that unity is not a destination,

It's a journey, that requires constant navigation.

We must constantly challenge ourselves, and society,

To ensure that we're moving towards, true equality.

We must be aware of, the subtle and overt biases,

And actively work to dismantle, these discriminatory practices.

We must be willing to learn, and to change,

For true unity, requires a range.

We must be willing to listen, to understand,

To the perspectives, of those who are different from our own land.

We must be willing to empathize, and to act,

For true unity, requires a pact.

A pact to work together, towards a common goal,

A world where ethnic divides, are no more, and the human soul

Is celebrated, respected, and honored,

For it is in this, that true unity is formed.

But let us not forget, that unity is not just a ideal,

It's a practice, that requires perseverance, and a will.

We must constantly remind ourselves, and each other,

That unity is not a destination, but a journey like no other.

We must be willing to put in the effort, and to take the lead,

To make sure that all voices are heard, and that all are in need.

We must be willing to make mistakes, and to learn from them,

For true unity, requires an open mind, and a heart that is warm.

We must be willing to challenge the status quo, and to stand up,

For those who are marginalized, and to fill up

The gaps that exist, in our society,

For true unity, requires a sense of community.

A community that works together, towards a common goal,

A world where ethnic divides, are no more, and the human soul

Is celebrated, respected, and honored,

For it is in this, that true unity is formed.

But let us not forget, that true unity, goes beyond mere tolerance,

It requires active acceptance, and an embrace of diversity.

We must learn to see the value, in different perspectives,

And to celebrate the richness, that cultural diversity brings us.

We must strive to create, an inclusive society,

Where everyone feels safe, and can thrive with dignity.

We must work to dismantle, the structures of oppression,

That keep certain ethnic groups, from reaching true success.

We must listen to the voices, of those who are marginalized,

And work to amplify, their stories, and make them acknowledged.

We must challenge ourselves, to move beyond our comfort zones,

And actively work towards, a world, where ethnic divides, are overthrown.

So let us strive for unity, and let it be our quest,

To build a world, where ethnic divides, are put to rest.

For in the grand scheme of things, we're all but mere mortals,

But together, we can create a world, that is truly, truly immortal.

Let us strive for unity, in all that we do,

And let us remember, that it is only through unity, that we can truly breakthrough

The barriers of ethnicity, and create a world where all are truly free,

A world where ethnic divides, are no more, and true unity, is our destiny.

6. The Quest for Meaning: A Poem on Religion

In times of yore, when man first trod
Upon this earth, his spirit awed
By all the splendor that surrounds
He sought to comprehend, what lay beyond
And thus, religion was born.
A quest for meaning in the great unknown
A quest for answers, to the questions shown
A quest for purpose, in this mortal coil
A quest for solace, in life's tumultuous toil
And thus, religion was formed.
But as the ages passed, and man did grow
His understanding of the world, did also flow
And with that knowledge, came a change of heart
A questioning of doctrine, a fresh start
And thus, religion was reformed.
For some, the quest for truth did lead
To a path of faith, in one's creed
For others, the quest for truth did lead
To a path of reason, in what they did heed
And thus, religion was divided.
But though the paths may differ far
The quest for meaning, is what unites each star
For in the end, it matters not the name
Of the faith we follow, or the gods we claim
For all religions seek the same.
A connection to the divine

A sense of purpose, that is truly mine
A path to peace, in the chaotic fray
A hope for redemption, at the end of the day
And thus, religion endures.
And as long as man shall walk this earth
He will seek answers, of his spirit's worth
For we are all seekers, of that which is holy
And our quest for meaning, shall never truly be wholly
And thus, religion will always be.
But as our quest for truth does progress
We must be mindful of our own transgress
For in our zeal for righteousness
We may cause harm, and bring distress
And thus, religion can be corrupted.
For in the name of our belief
We may discriminate, and cause grief
We may impose our will, on those who differ
And in the process, create a schism, that may never wither
And thus, religion can be divisive.
But despite the faults, that may arise
Religion still holds the power to compromise
For in the face of great adversity
It can bring people together, in unity
And thus, religion can be unifying.
For though our beliefs may vary wide
Our common humanity, can still be our guide
For in the end, we all share the same plight
And in that shared struggle, we can find light
And thus, religion can be a source of hope.
So let us not be quick to judge or hate
For in our differences, lies much to appreciate

Let us seek understanding, and strive for peace

For in the end, love and compassion, shall never cease

And thus, religion can be a force for good.

As we continue on our quest for truth

Let us be open-minded, and not aloof

For the answers we seek, may come from unexpected sources

And in the end, it is love that truly endures.

But as we navigate the winding path

Of religion and its aftermath

We must be careful not to stray

From the principles that guide us, each and every day

For it is easy to become lost

In the fervor of religious fervor, at any cost

But true faith, is not a matter of blind belief

But a journey of self-discovery, and inner relief

And thus, religion can be personal.

For each of us must find our own way

To connect with the divine, in our own way

And though the journey may be long

The destination is worth the song

For in the end, it is not the doctrine or the creed

But the connection to something greater, that we truly need

And thus, religion is a journey.

But as we travel on this road

We must be mindful of the heavy load

Of the weight of history, and the tales of old

For they shape our understanding, and can be both bold

And thus, religion is a legacy.

But as the world changes, and new knowledge unfolds

We must have the courage, to let go of what we've been told

For true faith, means being open to change

And embracing new perspectives, that may seem strange
And thus, religion is a process.
So let us not be afraid, to question and explore
For in the quest for truth, we may discover more
About ourselves, and the world around
And in the end, true religion can be truly profound.
But as we seek to understand
The mysteries of the divine hand
We must not forget the human touch
For religion is not just about the holy, but also the hush
For in the end, it is not the gods we worship
But the way we treat each other, that truly matters
For the love and kindness we show
Is the true measure of our faith, and the seed we sow
And thus, religion is a call to action.
But as we strive to do good in this world
We must be mindful of the flag unfurled
For in the name of religion, much harm has been done
And we must not let history repeat, under the same sun
And thus, religion must be held accountable.
For true faith, means standing up for what is right
And speaking out against wrong, with all our might
It means being a force for change, and not just for peace
But for justice, equality, and an end to human suffering and cease
And thus, religion is a call to social justice.
So let us not be content, with the status quo
For there is much work to be done, and much to know
Let us be active in our faith, and not just in words
For true religion, is not just about faith, but also actions and deeds.
For in the end, it is not the gods we worship
But the way we treat each other, that truly matters

For the love and kindness we show
Is the true measure of our faith, and the seed we sow.
But as we strive to live our lives
In harmony with the divine, and all that thrives
We must remember that our quest is not just for us
But for all living things, and the planet that we trust
And thus, religion is an environmental call.
For in the end, we are not separate
From the natural world, but an integral part of it, complete
And our actions have consequences, far and wide
And it is our responsibility, to be a steward, and not to abide
By practices that harm, and cause destruction
For in the end, it is not just our own salvation
But the preservation of the earth, for future generations
That should be at the forefront of our religious considerations
And thus, religion is a call to sustainability.
But as we strive to live in balance
With the earth, and all its plants and animals
We must also strive for balance within
For true religion is not just about the external, but also the internal spin
For in the end, it is not just about the pursuit of the divine
But also the cultivation of the self, and the ability to align
Body, mind, and spirit, in harmony
For true religion, is a holistic journey, not just a solitary symphony
And thus, religion is a call to self-improvement.
So let us not just seek answers, in texts and creeds
But also within ourselves, and our own deeds
For true religion, is a lifelong journey, not a destination
And the path we choose, will determine the ultimate sensation.
But as we navigate this journey of faith
We must remember that it is not a solitary path

For in our quest for understanding, we must also seek connection

With those around us, and their own perception

And thus, religion is a call to community.

For in the end, it is not just about our own salvation

But also the well-being of our fellow human nation

And our actions must be guided by compassion

And empathy, for the struggles of our fellow companion

And thus, religion is a call to social responsibility.

For true faith means standing in solidarity

With the marginalized, and those experiencing poverty

It means fighting for justice, and against oppression

And working towards a world of equality, without suppression

And thus, religion is a call to social justice.

But as we strive to make a difference in this world

We must not forget, that the journey is never unfurled

For there will always be more to learn, more to do

And our quest for understanding, will always renew

And thus, religion is a never-ending journey.

So let us be open-minded, and not too proud

For in the quest for truth, there is always something new to be found

And though the path may be winding, and the destination unclear

The journey itself, is what gives life meaning, and brings cheer.

But as we journey on this path of faith

We must remember that it is not always a smooth ride

There will be times of doubt and uncertainty

When our beliefs will be tested, and our willpower will be in rarity

And thus, religion can be a challenge.

For in the end, the journey of faith is not a guarantee

Of a life without struggles, or a life without adversity

But it is the belief that there is something greater than ourselves

That gives us the strength to face the challenges, and the wealth

And thus, religion is a source of strength.

For in the darkest of times, when all seems lost

Religion can offer a sense of hope, at any cost

It can provide comfort, in the midst of pain

And give meaning, to the struggles we sustain

And thus, religion is a source of comfort.

But as we face the challenges, and the test of faith

We must also remember that it is not just about personal gain

For true religion is not just about seeking salvation for oneself

But also about making a difference, to help others, and to be oneself

And thus, religion is a call to service.

So let us not be afraid, to face the trials of faith

For they are the opportunities, to become stronger, and to be safe

Let us be active in our beliefs, and use them to make a difference

For true religion, is not just about personal salvation, but also social persistence.

But as we strive to make a difference in this world

We must remember that religion is not just about words

It is not just about beliefs, or doctrines and creeds

It is about the way we live our lives, and the actions we lead

And thus, religion is a call to ethical living.

For true faith means living in accordance

With the principles of compassion, and moral resonance

It means being a force for good, and not just for peace

But for righteousness, and the pursuit of a life that is truly release

And thus, religion is a call to moral responsibility.

For in the end, it is not just about salvation in the afterlife

But also about living a good life, here and now, with no strife

For true religion is not just about the promise of a future reward

But about leading an ethical life, and being a force for good, evermore.

But as we strive to live an ethical life

We must remember that it is not always free from strife

For the path of righteousness is not always clear

And the choices we make, can bring us fear

And thus, religion is a call to moral discernment.

For true faith means making difficult choices

And standing up for what is right, even when our voices are hushed

It means being guided by our conscience, and not just by tradition

And being willing to question, and seek a deeper understanding, with conviction

And thus, religion is a call to moral autonomy.

So let us not be content, with simply going through the motions

For true religion is not just about following rules and devotions

It is about living an ethical life, and making a difference

For the betterment of ourselves and all others, with persistence.

But as we strive to live an ethical life

And make a difference in this world of strife

We must remember that religion is not just about us

But also about the interconnectedness of all living things, and the trust

And thus, religion is a call to interconnectivity.

For true faith means recognizing that we are not alone

That we are all connected, and share a common home

It means understanding that our actions have an impact

On the environment, and on the lives of others, and that's a fact

And thus, religion is a call to ecological responsibility.

For in the end, it is not just about our own salvation

But also about the well-being of all creation

And our actions must be guided by respect

For the balance of nature, and the earth's ecosystem, that we must protect

And thus, religion is a call to environmental stewardship.

But as we strive to make a difference, and do our part

We must remember that religion is not just about the head start

It is also about the heart and the spirit

And the connection to something greater, that we inherit

And thus, religion is a call to spiritual connectedness.

For true faith means fostering a connection

To something greater than ourselves, and this reflection

It means seeking a deeper understanding, of the purpose and meaning of life

And cultivating a sense of wonder and awe, without any strife

And thus, religion is a call to spiritual growth.

So let us not just seek answers, in texts and creeds

But also within ourselves, and our own deeds

For true religion, is a lifelong journey, not a destination

And the path we choose, will determine the ultimate sensation.

But as we journey on this path of faith,

we must remember that it is not always a smooth ride,

there will be times when our beliefs will be challenged,

and our faith will be put to the test, and it will be hard to decide.

And thus, religion is a call to resilience.

For true faith means having the courage to face,

the difficulties and uncertainties, with grace,

it means being able to hold on, to what we believe,

even in the face of doubt, and disbelief.

And thus, religion is a call to perseverance.

For in the end, the journey of faith is not always easy,

and it requires a strong will and determination, to be free,

from the struggles and hardships, that come our way,

and to keep moving forward, and not to sway.

And thus, religion is a call to determination.

But as we strive to live a life of faith,

we must remember that it is not just about personal gain,

for true religion is not just about seeking salvation for oneself,

but also about making a difference, to help others, and to be oneself.

And thus, religion is a call to service.

So let us not be afraid, to face the trials of faith,

for they are the opportunities, to become stronger, and to be safe,

let us be active in our beliefs, and use them to make a difference,

for true religion, is not just about personal salvation, but also social persistence.

But as we journey on this path of faith,

we must remember that it is not just about us,

for religion is not just about personal salvation,

but also about the greater good, and the community's elevation.

And thus, religion is a call to community.

For true faith means being a part of something greater,

than ourselves, and working together, to create a better picture,

it means being connected to others, and being a support,

in times of need, and being a beacon of hope, to resort.

And thus, religion is a call to social connection.

For in the end, the journey of faith is not just about personal growth,

but also about the collective well-being, and the community's flow,

it's about working together, to create a better world,

and lifting each other up, and being a part of a whole.

And thus, religion is a call to collective action.

But as we strive to make a difference, in this world,

we must remember that religion is not just about words,

it is not just about beliefs, or doctrines and creeds,

it is about the way we live our lives, and the actions we lead.

7. The Placebo Paradox: A Tale of Healing and Challenges

In the realm of medicine, a tale doth unfold

Of a phenomenon known as the placebo, oft bold

A mere sugar pill, or saline shot with nought

Yet the power to heal, doth oft leave us fraught

For the mind is a labyrinth, full of twists and turns

And the placebo effect, doth show us the mind's concerns

For the power of belief, doth oft outstrip

The power of drugs, a concept most equivocal

The placebo effect, a conundrum most perplexing

For the mind's ability to heal, oft leaves us guessing

How does the mere belief in a treatment, bring forth

Healing, when the treatment itself, is of no worth

But the power of the mind, doth not stop at the placebo

For the power of the mind, doth oft outlast and outflow

The power of drugs, and the power of the sword

For the mind is the ultimate healing force, never ignored

Thus let us embrace the placebo effect, not as a foe

But as a testament to the mind's power, and let it flow

For the power of belief, doth oft bring forth the cure

And the mind's ability to heal, doth oft endure.

But the placebo effect, doth raise a moral quandary

For the use of sugar pills, doth seem most contrary

To the Hippocratic Oath, to do no harm

But the power of the mind, doth oft out-swarm

The potential for harm, in the use of a placebo

For the power of belief, doth oft bring forth the ego

And the ego, a force most formidable

Can bring forth both good and bad, most formidable

Thus the use of placebo, doth raise a moral question

For the power of the mind, doth oft bring forth obsession

And the obsession for a cure, doth oft cloud the mind

Leaving the patient, in a state most unrefined

But the placebo effect, doth also bring forth hope

For the power of the mind, doth oft give the patient scope

To believe in a cure, and to fight the disease

And the power of hope, doth oft bring forth ease

So let us embrace the placebo effect, not with disdain

But with caution and thought, and let it remain

A tool in the arsenal of medicine, a force to be reckoned

But one that must be wielded, with the utmost discretion.

But the placebo effect, doth not only reside

In the realm of medicine, where it's often espied

It doth permeate our lives, in ways most subtle

For the power of belief, doth oft bring forth the subtle

In our relationships, our work, and our dreams

The placebo effect, doth oft seem

To play a role, in the outcomes we attain

For the power of belief, doth oft bring forth the gain

But the placebo effect, doth also bring forth loss

For the power of belief, doth oft bring forth the dross

Of disappointment, and unfulfilled desire

For the power of belief, doth oft bring forth the mire

So let us be mindful, of the placebo effect

And use its power, with the utmost respect

For the power of belief, doth oft shape our fate

And the power of the mind, doth oft create.

But the placebo effect, doth not only reside in the realm of physical health

But also in our mental and emotional wealth
For the power of belief, doth oft shape our reality
And the mind's ability to heal, doth oft bring forth serenity
In the face of adversity, the placebo effect doth show
The power of the mind, to let go
Of negative thoughts, and to embrace positivity
For the power of belief, doth oft bring forth tranquility
But the placebo effect, doth also bring forth its own set of challenges
For the power of belief, doth oft bring forth the balances
Between the power of the mind, and the power of the heart
For the power of belief, doth oft bring forth a delicate art
Thus let us embrace the placebo effect, not as a panacea
But as a tool, to be used with discretion and criteria
For the power of belief, doth oft shape our lives
And the power of the mind, doth oft bring forth thrive.
But the placebo effect, doth not only reside in the realm of the individual
But also in the society, it doth dwell
For the power of belief, doth oft shape the collective
And the mind's ability to heal, doth oft bring forth the collective
In the face of societal issues, the placebo effect doth show
The power of the collective mind, to let go
Of negative stereotypes, and to embrace diversity
For the power of belief, doth oft bring forth unity
But the placebo effect, doth also bring forth its own set of challenges
For the power of belief, doth oft bring forth the balances
Between the power of the collective mind, and the power of the individual
For the power of belief, doth oft bring forth a delicate equilibrium
Thus let us embrace the placebo effect, not as a utopia
But as a tool, to be used with fairness and criteria
For the power of belief, doth oft shape our society
And the power of the collective mind, doth oft bring forth prosperity

8. Etched in Stone: Reflections on Life, Death, and Legacy

Upon a visit to graveyards so still and serene,

Where tombstones stand in solemn rows, a silent, somber scene,

One cannot help but ponder on the transience of life,

And question the existence of an afterlife.

Amidst the mossy headstones, the crumbling masonry,

Lies a reminder of our own mortality,

For as the seasons change, and flowers wilt and fade,

So too do we, in time, succumb to death's cold shade.

But is there something more beyond this mortal coil,

A spirit that persists, a soul that does not spoil?

Or are we but mere vessels, empty and forlorn,

Fated to return to dust, once our brief lives are done?

As one wanders through the graveyard, surrounded by the dead,

One cannot help but contemplate the nature of the soul,

And question the existence of an afterlife, or the lack thereof,

And whether or not we'll find some solace at the end, or just a gaping hole.

For some, the thought of death brings a sense of finality,

A feeling of despair, a loss of all reality,

While others find comfort in the thought of eternal rest,

And a reunion with loved ones, who have passed the mortal test.

But whether or not there's life beyond this earthly sphere,

One thing is certain, death is always near,

So let us live our lives to the fullest, with purpose and with grace,

And make the most of every moment, before we take our final place.

In graveyards, we find a reflection of our own mortality,

A reminder to cherish every day, and to live with humility,

For in the end, all that remains is memories and stone,

Etched with our name, and all that we have known.

And as the mists of time obscure the memories of the past,

And the headstones crumble, yielding to the forces of the blast,

We must remember that though our physical form may fade,

Our legacy, our impact, will forever be engraved.

In graveyards, we find a testament to human history,

A reminder of the lives that have been, and the stories they carry,

For every grave is a story, a tale of love and loss,

Of triumphs and tragedies, and the human cost.

But graveyards are not just a place of sorrow and despair,

They are also a place of hope, of healing and repair,

For in these hallowed grounds, we find solace in the thought,

That though our loved ones may be gone, their memories will be sought.

So let us visit graveyards not with fear or with dread,

But with reverence, and a sense of gratitude for the dead,

For they have paved the way for us, and shown us how to live,

And in their passing, they have taught us how to give.

So let us honor the dead, and keep their memories alive,

For though they may be gone, their spirits will always thrive,

For in graveyards, we find a connection to the past,

And a sense of hope for the future, that forever will last.

As we lay flowers on the graves, and whisper words of grief,

We also honor the lives that were lived, and find relief,

For in visiting graveyards, we come to understand,

That death is not an end, but a part of life's grand plan.

For every grave tells a story, a chapter in the book of time,

Of a life that was lived, and a soul that once did shine,

And as we pay our respects, we come to realize,

That death may take us from this world, but it cannot take our ties.

For love and memories, they live on and on,

And though our loved ones may be gone, they will forever be drawn,

Into our hearts, and etched upon our minds,

For they are a part of us, and will forever be entwined.

So let us visit graveyards, and pay our respects,

For in these hallowed grounds, we find peace and deep respect,

For the lives that were lived, and the souls that once did soar,

For in death, they may be gone, but they are forevermore.

In graveyards, we find a lesson, a reminder to be true,

To ourselves and to others, in all that we pursue,

For in the end, it's not our possessions or our fame,

That will mark our legacy, but the love that we proclaim.

So let us make the most of every day, and cherish every breath,

For we never know when our time on earth will come to an end,

And let us leave behind a trail of love, a trail of light,

That will guide those who come after us, through the darkest night.

For in visiting graveyards, we are reminded that life is fleeting,

And that we must make the most of every moment, without hesitation or cheating,

For time waits for no one, and death will come for us all,

But if we live with purpose, our legacy will never fall.

So let us visit graveyards, not with fear or with despair,

But with gratitude, for the lives that were lived, and the love that they shared,

For in these hallowed grounds, we find a connection to the past,

And a sense of hope for the future, that forever will last.

In graveyards, we find a reminder to cherish our time,

For death is not the end, but a transition, a climb,

To a realm unknown, a mystery yet to unfold,

But one that we should not fear, for it is not a story that's told.

For death is not a punishment, nor a curse,

But a natural process, that happens to us all, in verse,

It is the end of a chapter, the close of a book,

But not the end of the story, just a new path to look.

And as we stand before the graves, in silent contemplation,

We understand that life is but a fleeting sensation,

A journey that we undertake, a path that we must tread,

But one that is worth taking, for it is the journey of the dead.

So let us visit graveyards, not with tears and with sorrow,

But with reverence and gratitude, for the gift of tomorrow,

For in these hallowed grounds, we find a connection to the past,

And a sense of hope for the future, that forever will last.

And as we leave the graveyard, and return to our daily lives,

We carry with us the lessons and the memories, that the dead still gives,

For in visiting graveyards, we are reminded of our own mortality,

And the preciousness of life, and the importance of humility.

For every grave is a reminder, that our time on earth is but a flicker,

A momentary spark, in the grand scheme of things, a glimmer,

And it is up to us, to make the most of every day,

To live with purpose, and to pave the way.

So let us visit graveyards, not with fear or with dread,

But with reverence, and a sense of gratitude for the dead,

For they have shown us, that life is but a fleeting thing,

But one that is worth living, with love and with meaning.

So let us honor the dead, and keep their memories alive,

For though they may be gone, their spirits will always thrive,

For in graveyards, we find a connection to the past,

And a sense of hope for the future, that forever will last.

In graveyards, we find a connection to our ancestors,

A reminder of the history, and the stories of the ventures,

For every grave tells a tale, a chapter in the book of time,

Of the struggles and the triumphs, of the lives that once did shine.

And as we walk among the graves, we come to understand,

That death is not an end, but a part of a greater plan,

For as the old pass on, the new is born,

And the cycle of life continues, in an eternal morn.

In graveyards, we find a reflection of our own mortality,

A reminder that our time on earth is but a temporary reality,

And that we must make the most of every moment, every breath,

For death is not the end, but a step towards something beyond death.

And as we wander through the graveyard, surrounded by the dead,

We come to understand that life is fragile, and that we must tread,

With care and compassion, and with an open heart,

For we never know when our own time will depart.

Upon the hallowed grounds of graveyards so still,

Where tombstones stand in solemn rows, a silent chill,

We're reminded of our own mortality and plight,

And that in death, we're equal, free from wealth or height.

Amidst the mossy headstones, the crumbling masonry,

Lies a testament to human frailty, a history,

For as the seasons change, and flowers wilt and fade,

So too do we, in time, succumb to death's cold shade.

But in these hallowed grounds, we find a sense of peace,

A reminder that in death, all conflicts cease,

For rich or poor, famous or unknown,

We all share the same fate, and return to the earth, alone.

So let us visit graveyards, with an open mind and heart,

And learn from the lessons, that death and time impart.

For in these hallowed grounds, we find a connection to the past,

And a sense of hope for the future, that forever will last.

And as we leave the graveyard, and return to our daily lives,

Let us carry with us the lessons, that the dead still gives.

9. The Power and Beauty of Language: A Poetic Exploration

In ancient times, when man first learned to speak,

Language was but a primitive tool, unique.

A means to share one's thoughts and needs with others,

But as time passed, it became so much more than that, brothers.

With language, man was able to create,

To build, to dream, to contemplate.

It allowed us to transcend our earthly bounds,

And explore the vast expanse of knowledge found.

But language is not just a tool for expression,

It shapes the very way we perceive the world's dimension.

It limits our understanding and our truth,

For the words we use can warp our perception, uncouth.

And as society evolves and language changes,

We must be mindful of its dangers and its ranges.

For the words we choose can either liberate or enslave,

And the power of language should never be taken for granted, brave.

So let us use our words with care and thought,

To build a better world, where all are taught,

The beauty and complexity of language,

And its ability to connect, to heal, and to advance.

But language is not just a tool for the mind,

It is also a tool for the heart and the soul combined.

It allows us to express love and affection,

And to form bonds that are deep and true, without objection.

Language is a window to the human experience,

It allows us to understand and to make sense.

Of the world around us and the people we meet,

And to connect on a level that is both profound and discreet.

But language can also be used as a weapon,

To harm, to divide and to create tension.

It is up to us to choose our words with care,

And to be mindful of the impact they bear.

Language is a reflection of our humanity,

Of our hopes, our fears, and our insanity.

It is a tool that we must use responsibly,

To create a world that is just and free.

So let us embrace the complexity and beauty of language,

And use it to build a world that is fair and true.

For it is through our words that we can create change,

And make the world a better place for me and you.

But as we use language to communicate,

We must not forget its innate state.

Language is not only a tool for expression,

But also an art, a beauty that requires attention.

Poetry and literature, music and song,

All use language to create something strong.

Something that touches the heart and the soul,

And leaves a lasting impression, that's whole.

Language is not just about conveying information,

But also about evoking emotion and imagination.

It's about connecting with others on a deeper level,

And understanding the beauty of life, that's revel.

Language is not just a means to an end,

But an end in itself, a journey to befriend.

As we continue to use it to express ourselves,

Let us not forget its beauty and its wealth.

So let us use language not just to communicate,

But also to appreciate, to create and to celebrate.

For it is through language that we can truly understand,

The beauty and complexity of the world, and take a stand.

But language is not just a human construct,

It is also a reflection of our culture and context.

Different languages and dialects,

Are a manifestation of our history and cultural respects.

Language is a means of preserving our heritage,

A link to our past and a guide to our future.

It is a symbol of our identity and diversity,

A connection to our roots and our destiny.

However, as the world becomes increasingly globalized,

We must be mindful of the impact of language on marginalized.

Minoritized languages and dialects are at risk of extinction,

A loss of diversity, culture, and tradition that's a conviction.

We must strive to preserve and promote,

Languages and dialects, as we navigate the scope.

For they are an essential part of our shared humanity,

And a reflection of our unique and diverse community.

So let us use language not just to communicate,

But also to understand and appreciate.

The beauty of diversity and the richness of culture,

And the importance of preserving them for future.

But as we delve deeper into the complexity of language,

We must also consider the ethical implications of its usage and advantage.

For language has the power to shape our understanding of the world and ourselves,

And can be used to justify oppression and marginalization, it delves.

The language we use, the words we choose,

Can perpetuate harmful stereotypes and biases we refuse.

It is our responsibility to recognize and challenge,

The ways in which language is used to marginalize and mishandle.

We must strive to create a more inclusive language,

That reflects the diversity and complexity of our world and its range.

A language that promotes equality and respect,

And challenges systems of oppression, that we reject.

So let us use language not just to communicate,

But also to challenge and to change.

Let us use our words to create a more just world,

And to empower those who are marginalized and unfurled.

Language is a powerful tool, that can be used for good or ill,

It's up to us to choose how we use it, and to make sure that it's still,

A means of connection and understanding, and a reflection of our humanity,

And to ensure that it serves to uplift, and not to oppress or insanity.

But language is not just a human invention,

It is also a product of evolution.

It has evolved over time, shaped by culture and context,

And it continues to evolve, as society and technology advance.

New words are created, old words fall out of use,

Language adapts to the changing world and its views.

It is a living and dynamic thing,

That reflects the ever-changing nature of humanity and everything.

And as language evolves, so must we,

To keep up with its changes and nuances, it's due.

We must be open to new ways of communicating,

And to understanding the perspectives of others, it's worth noting.

So let us embrace the evolution of language,

And use it to connect and to understand.

Let us use it to create a more inclusive world,

And to promote understanding, empathy and to expand.

Language is a constantly evolving tool,

That has the power to connect, to create, and to change the rules.

Let us use it to its fullest potential,

And to make the world a better place, it's essential.

But as we use language to connect and to create,

We must also be aware of its limitations and its fate.

For language, as powerful as it may be,

Is still a human construct, and it is not infallible, you see.

Language is a tool, but it is not the only tool,

There are other ways to communicate and to be cool.

Nonverbal communication, body language, and emotions,

Can convey meaning and understanding, and it's not just notions.

We must be aware that language is not always enough,

To truly understand and connect, it may be tough.

For language is a tool, but it is not the only tool,

And it is not the end-all and be-all, it's not a rule.

So let us use language, but let us not rely on it,

Let us use it in conjunction with other tools, that fit.

For true understanding and connection,

Is not just about language, but also about other forms of expression.

In conclusion, language is a powerful and complex tool,

It has the power to connect, to create and to change the rules.

Let us use it wisely, and with a deep understanding,

And let us not forget its beauty, its evolution, and its impact on humanity and

everything impending.

10. Eternal Embrace: A Poem on the True Nature of Love

In times of yore, when hearts were pure,

And love was nought but true,

A bond was forged, a love was stored,

A flame that burned anew.

But as the ages came and went,

And man's corruption grew,

The meaning of true love was bent,

A thing of nought but woo.

For love is not just fluttering hearts,

Or stolen kisses sweet,

It's not just words that play a part,

But actions that entreat.

It's sacrifice and dedication,

The will to see it through,

It's standing by in adulation,

And being there for you.

For love is not a game to play,

Or trifle to discard,

It's a commitment come what may,

A bond that's hard to guard.

So let us cherish love's true form,

And hold it in our hearts,

For it is the one thing that keeps us warm,

And sets our souls apart.

In this love we find our worth,

Our purpose and our guide,

It is the light that guides us forth,
Through life's tumultuous tide.
So let us love with all our might,
And let our love be true,
For in this love, we find our light,
And all our dreams come true.
But love is not just for the young,
Or for the fair of face,
It's not a thing to be hung,
Upon a lover's grace.
For love is not a thing of looks,
But of the heart and soul,
It's not a book of empty nooks,
But a story yet untold.
Love is not a thing of chance,
But a choice we make each day,
It's not a circumstance,
But a commitment we convey.
It's not just a feeling to possess,
But a journey to embark,
It's not a thing of happiness,
But a fire that never dark.
For love is not a thing of ease,
But a path that's often rough,
It's not a thing of guarantees,
But a challenge to be tough.
But in this love we find our strength,
Our courage and our guide,
It's the fire that lights our length,
And the anchor that keeps us tied.
So let us love with all our might,

And let our love be true,
For in this love, we find our light,
And all our dreams come true.
Love is the greatest force of all,
That gives our lives true meaning,
It's the one thing that stands tall,
Through all life's joy and leaning.
So let us cherish love's true form,
And hold it in our hearts,
For it is the one thing that keeps us warm,
And sets our souls apart.
But love is not just for ourselves,
It's not a thing of gain,
It's not a thing to hoard or shelve,
But to share and to sustain.
For love is not a thing of greed,
But of compassion and of care,
It's not a thing of selfish need,
But of selfless service to share.
It's not a thing to take or hold,
But to give and to inspire,
It's not a thing to be controlled,
But to flow like a river.
For love is not a thing of bounds,
But of infinity and grace,
It's not a thing of earthly rounds,
But of eternal embrace.
And in this love we find our peace,
Our joy and our salvation,
It's the one thing that will never cease,
And our hearts' true revelation.

So let us love with all our hearts,
And let our love be pure,
For in this love, we'll find the start,
Of a journey that will endure.
Love is the one thing that we need,
In this world of pain and strife,
It's the one thing that will lead,
To a life of love and light.
But love is not just for the present,
Or for the days ahead,
It's not a thing that's easily spent,
Or something to be shed.
For love is not a thing of time,
But of eternity and space,
It's not a thing of reason or rhyme,
But of mystery and grace.
It's not a thing that can be measured,
Or quantified with ease,
It's not a thing that can be treasured,
Or kept within a case.
For love is not a thing of things,
But a force that moves the soul,
It's not a thing that can have strings,
But a freedom that makes us whole.
And in this love we find our freedom,
Our purpose and our guide,
It's the one thing that will lead us,
To the truth that we can't hide.
So let us love with all our hearts,
And let our love be true,
For in this love, we'll find the start,

Of a journey that will renew.
Love is the one thing that we need,
In this world of fear and hate,
It's the one thing that will lead,
To a life of love and fate.
So let us cherish love's true form,
And hold it in our hearts,
For it is the one thing that keeps us warm,
And sets our souls apart.
But love is not just for the good times,
Or for the days of joy,
It's not a thing that only shines,
When everything's deployed.
For love is not a thing of ease,
But of strength in times of trial,
It's not a thing of guarantees,
But of perseverance and denial.
It's not a thing that can be swayed,
By doubts or fears or pain,
It's not a thing that can be played,
Like a game or in disdain.
For love is not a thing of might,
But a power that's beyond,
It's not a thing that can take flight,
But a treasure that's always fond.
And in this love we find our courage,
Our hope and our salvation,
It's the one thing that will encourage,
us to rise above the nation.
So let us love with all our might,
And let our love be true,

For in this love, we'll find the fight,
To overcome the blue.
Love is the one thing that we need,
In this world of pain and fear,
It's the one thing that will lead,
To a life of love and cheer.
But love is not just for the perfect,
Or for the flawless and the pure,
It's not a thing that's to be kept,
For the elite and the demure.
For love is not a thing of class,
But of acceptance and of grace,
It's not a thing of looking past,
But of seeing the beauty in each face.
It's not a thing that can be earned,
By wealth or fame or pride,
It's not a thing that can be spurned,
Or cast aside.
For love is not a thing of choice,
But a gift that's freely given,
It's not a thing of one's own voice,
But a bond that's meant for heaven.
And in this love we find our acceptance,
Our belonging and our guide,
It's the one thing that will bring us,
To a life that's truly tried.
So let us love with all our hearts,
And let our love be true,
For in this love, we'll find the start,
Of a journey that's meant for two.
Love is the one thing that we need,

In this world of hate and war,

It's the one thing that will lead,

To a life of love and more.

But love is not just for the present,

Or for the days ahead,

It's not a thing that's easily spent,

Or something to be shed.

For love is not a thing of time,

But of eternity and space,

It's not a thing of reason or rhyme,

But of mystery and grace.

It's not a thing that can be grasped,

Or fully understood,

It's not a thing that can be clasped,

Or kept in the hood.

For love is not a thing at all,

But a force that moves the heart,

It's not a thing that can be called,

But a feeling that sets us apart.

And in this love we find our purpose,

Our meaning and our guide,

It's the one thing that will surface,

When all else has subsided.

So let us love with all our being,

And let our love be true,

For in this love, we'll find the meaning,

Of a life that's meant for two.

Love is the one thing that we need,

In this world of strife and pain,

It's the one thing that will lead,

To a life of love and gain.

But love is not just for the human,
Or for the physical realm,
It's not a thing that's to be done,
By the weak or the helm.
For love is not a thing of flesh,
But of spirit and of soul,
It's not a thing of mortal mesh,
But of an eternal whole.
It's not a thing that can be grasped,
Or fully understood,
It's not a thing that can be clasped,
Or kept in the hood.
For love is not a thing of self,
But of the divine and pure,
It's not a thing of human wealth,
But of the eternal lure.
And in this love we find our salvation,
Our redemption and our guide,
It's the one thing that will bring us,
To the other side.
So let us love with all our hearts,
And let our love be true,
For in this love, we'll find the start,
Of an eternal journey anew.
Love is the one thing that we need,
In this world of darkness and night,
It's the one thing that will lead,
To a life of love and light.
So let us cherish love's true form,
And hold it in our hearts,
For it is the one thing that keeps us warm,

And sets our souls apart.
For love is not a thing of time,
But of eternity and space,
It's not a thing of reason or rhyme,
But of mystery and grace.
It's not a thing that can be measured,
Or quantified with ease,
It's not a thing that can be treasured,
Or kept within a case.
For love is not a thing of things,
But a force that moves the soul,
It's not a thing that can have strings,
But a freedom that makes us whole.
And in this love we find our freedom,
Our purpose and our guide,
It's the one thing that will lead us,
To the truth that we can't hide.
So let us love with all our hearts,
And let our love be true,
For in this love, we'll find the start,
Of a journey that will renew.
But love is not just for the happy,
Or for the days of mirth,
It's not a thing that's always snappy,
Or stays on the surface of earth.
For love is not a thing of smiles,
But of tears and pain and fears,
It's not a thing that goes the miles,
Without facing the darkest fears.
It's not a thing that can be forced,
Or controlled by will or might,

It's not a thing that can be sourced,
Or hidden from the light.
For love is not a thing of self,
But of the other and the whole,
It's not a thing of gaining wealth,
But of giving and making whole.
And in this love we find our meaning,
Our purpose and our guide,
It's the one thing that will bring us,
To the other side.
So let us love with all our hearts,
And let our love be true,
For in this love, we'll find the start,
Of a journey that's meant to be true,
But love is not just for the chosen,
Or for the privileged few,
It's not a thing that's to be frozen,
Or kept away from view.
For love is not a thing of class,
But of the open and the kind,
It's not a thing of looking back,
But of reaching out the mind.
It's not a thing that can be earned,
By wealth or fame or pride,
It's not a thing that can be spurned,
Or cast aside.
For love is not a thing of choice,
But a gift that's freely given,
It's not a thing of one's own voice,
But a bond that's meant for heaven.
And in this love we find our acceptance,

Our belonging and our guide,
It's the one thing that will bring us,
To a life that's truly tried.
But love is not just for the fleeting,
Or for the moments in time,
It's not a thing that's incompletely,
Or left behind.
For love is not a thing of now,
But of the past and future too,
It's not a thing of taking vow,
But of growing and renew.
It's not a thing that can be forced,
Or made to fit a mold,
It's not a thing that can be divorced,
Or bought or sold.
For love is not a thing of possession,
But of connection and of trust,
It's not a thing of obsession,
But of respect and mutual must.
And in this love we find our growth,
Our evolution and our guide,
It's the one thing that will show,
The beauty in the other side.
So let us love with all our being,
And let our love be true,
For in this love, we'll find the meaning,
Of a journey that's meant for me and you.
Love is the one thing that we need,
In this world of change and shift,
It's the one thing that will lead,
To a life of love and lift.

So let us cherish love's true form,
And hold it in our hearts,
For it is the one thing that keeps us warm,
And sets our souls apart.

11. The Grand Enigma of Life

Life, a concept so grand and profound,
An enigma that continues to astound.
With each breath and every beating heart,
We are reminded of our fleeting part.
The origins of life, a question that plagues,
Scientists and philosophers for ages.
From the primordial soup to the spark of a cell,
The evolution of life is a tale to tell.
But what is the purpose of this existence?
Is it to simply persist in resistance?
Or is there a higher meaning, a reason for all,
That transcends the physical, the intangible call?
The complexity of life is a marvel to behold,
From the microscopic to the stories untold.
The beauty of nature, the diversity of form,
All part of the tapestry, the cosmic norm.
And yet, amidst the grandeur and splendour,
There is also pain, suffering, befuddling.
The cycle of birth and death, the constant change,
Reminds us of the impermanence and strange.
But perhaps it is in this impermanence,
That we find true significance.
For it is in the fleeting moments,
That we truly live.
So let us cherish each day,
And make the most of the time we have,
For life is a precious gift,

And the only one we have.
So let us live with purpose,
And make our mark on the world,
For it is in the living,
That the true meaning unfurled.
For in the end, life is but a journey,
A path we all must tread,
And it is in this journey,
That we find our ultimate end.
But the end is not the final destination,
For the journey continues on, in a new sensation.
The cycle of life and death is eternal,
And in it, we find the true essence of being.
For in death, we find new beginnings,
A transformation of energy, never ending.
The atoms that make up our being,
Will continue on, in a new form, fleeting.
So let us not fear death,
For it is but a natural progression.
Let us embrace the mystery and unknown,
For in it, we find true liberation.
For in the end, life is but a fleeting moment,
A mere blip in the grand scheme of things.
But in that moment, we have the power,
To leave our mark, to spread our wings.
So let us live with purpose,
And make the most of the time we have.
For life is a precious gift,
And the only one we have.
So let us embrace the beauty and the pain,
For in it, we find the true essence of life.

For it is in the living,

That we find our purpose and our strife.

For life is an epic journey,

A tale that will be told.

And it is in this journey,

That we find our ultimate goal.

So let us not waste a single moment,

For time is a precious commodity.

Let us make our mark on the world,

And leave a legacy of humility.

For in the end, it is not the material things,

That we will be remembered for.

It is the kindness we've shown,

The love that we've adored.

So let us strive for love and compassion,

For it is the true essence of life.

Let us be a beacon of hope,

In the midst of all the strife.

For life is a precious gift,

Given to us but for a while.

Let us make the most of it,

With a smile.

For in the end, it is not the length of our days,

That will be remembered,

But the impact we've made,

On the hearts that we've touched, forever.

For life is an epic journey,

A grand adventure, we all must face.

Let us make it a tale worth telling,

And leave our mark on this place.

Let us not be content with mediocrity,

But strive for greatness, in all that we do.

Let us push the boundaries,

And see what we are truly capable of.

For life is a canvas,

Waiting to be painted.

Let us make our mark,

With colors vibrant and vaunted.

For in the end, it is not the destination,

But the journey that truly matters.

Let us make the most of each day,

And leave no stone unturned, no chapter untattered.

Let us not be afraid of the unknown,

But embrace it with open arms.

For in the unknown, we find true growth,

And unlock the secrets that keep us from harm.

For life is a mystery,

A puzzle yet to be solved.

Let us strive to understand it,

And evolve.

Let us not be swayed by societal pressure,

Or the expectations of others.

Let us live our own lives,

And be true to ourselves, like no other.

For in the end, it is not the opinions of others,

That will define us.

It is the choices we make,

And the paths we choose, that will shine us.

Let us not be afraid to take risks,

Or to chart our own course.

For it is in taking risks,

That we find true power and force.

For life is a winding road,

With many twists and turns.

Let us make the most of it,

And learn from every lesson.

For in the end, it is not the destination,

But the journey that truly matters.

Let us make the most of each day,

And leave no stone unturned, no chapter untattered.

Let us not take a single moment for granted,

For time is fleeting, and it may not be.

Let us cherish the people we love,

And make the most of their company.

For in the end, it is not the material possessions,

That will bring us true happiness.

It is the love and connections,

That we make with others, that will make us bliss.

Let us not be afraid to dream,

And to chase our wildest aspirations.

For it is in reaching for the stars,

That we find true inspiration.

For life is a journey,

A path of self-discovery.

Let us make the most of it,

And find our own way, with bravery.

Let us not be blinded by the illusions of this world,

But strive to see the truth, in all that surrounds us.

For in the quest for knowledge and understanding,

We find true freedom and thus.

For in the end, it is not the things we acquire,

But the wisdom we gain, that will truly last.

Let us seek the answers to life's great mysteries,

And let our minds forever surpass.
Let us not be afraid to question,
To challenge the status quo.
For in doing so, we open ourselves,
To new perspectives and growth.
Let us not be content with the superficial,
But strive to dig deeper and find meaning.
For in the quest for understanding,
We find true fulfillment and leaning.
For in the end, it is not the surface-level things,
But the depth of our being, that will truly last.
Let us seek to understand the complexities,
And let our souls forever surpass.
Let us not be afraid to explore,
To wander and be curious.
For in doing so, we open ourselves,
To new experiences and opportunities.
For life is a journey of exploration,
A path that is unique to each one.
Let us make the most of it,
And find our own way, under the sun.
Let us not be limited by our own beliefs,
But strive to expand our understanding.
For in the quest for knowledge and awareness,
We find true wisdom and landing.
For in the end, it is not the things we know,
But the depth of our knowing, that will truly last.
Let us seek to understand the intricacies,
And let our hearts forever surpass.
Let us not be afraid to question,
To challenge our own assumptions.

For in doing so, we open ourselves,

To new possibilities and solutions.

Let us not be content with the ordinary,

But strive to reach for the extraordinary.

For in the quest for greatness,

We find true purpose and destiny.

For in the end, it is not the things we accomplish,

But the depth of our ambition, that will truly last.

Let us seek to achieve the impossible,

And let our efforts forever surpass.

Let us not be afraid to dream,

To set our sights high and be bold.

For in doing so, we open ourselves,

To new possibilities and untold.

For life is a journey of aspirations,

A path that is unique to each one.

Let us make the most of it,

And find our own way, under the sun.

Let us not be constrained by our fears,

But strive to overcome them with courage.

For in the quest for bravery,

We find true strength and advantage.

For in the end, it is not the things we avoid,

But the depth of our courage, that will truly last.

Let us seek to face our fears,

And let our willpower forever surpass.

Let us not be afraid to take risks,

To step out of our comfort zone.

For in doing so, we open ourselves,

To new opportunities and unknown.

Let us not be limited by our limitations,

But strive to push beyond them with determination.

For in the quest for growth,

We find true potential and revelation.

For in the end, it is not the things we can't do,

But the depth of our determination, that will truly last.

Let us seek to break our own boundaries,

And let our aspirations forever surpass.

Let us not be afraid to fail,

To learn from our mistakes and grow.

For in doing so, we open ourselves,

To new opportunities and a brighter tomorrow.

Let us not be defined by our past,

But strive to create our own future.

For in the quest for self-determination,

We find true autonomy and suture.

For in the end, it is not the things that have happened,

But the depth of our willpower, that will truly last.

Let us seek to shape our own destiny,

And let our determination forever surpass.

Let us not be afraid to start anew,

To let go of the past and move on.

For in doing so, we open ourselves,

To new possibilities and a brighter dawn.

For life is a journey of self-creation,

A path that is unique to each one.

Let us make the most of it,

And find our own way, under the sun.

Let us not be held back by our doubts,

But strive to believe in ourselves and our abilities.

For in the quest for self-confidence,

We find true strength and capabilities.

For in the end, it is not the things we doubt,

But the depth of our belief, that will truly last.

Let us seek to trust in ourselves,

And let our self-confidence forever surpass.

Let us not be afraid to take action,

To put our plans into motion and strive.

For in doing so, we open ourselves,

To new possibilities and a fulfilling life.

For life is a journey of self-realization,

A path that is unique to each one.

Let us make the most of it,

And find our own way, under the sun.

Let us not be defined by our mistakes,

But strive to learn and grow from them.

For in the quest for self-improvement,

We find true wisdom and gem.

For in the end, it is not the things we did wrong,

But the depth of our self-awareness, that will truly last.

Let us seek to understand our own weaknesses,

And let our self-improvement forever surpass.

Let us not be afraid to admit our faults,

To take responsibility and make amends.

For in doing so, we open ourselves,

To new opportunities for growth and mends.

For life is a journey of self-reflection,

A path that is unique to each one.

Let us make the most of it,

And find our own way, under the sun.

For in the end, it is not the destination,

But the journey that truly matters.

Let us make the most of each day,

And leave our mark, in letters and splatters.
For life is an epic journey,
A tale of self-discovery and self-improvement.
Let us make the most of it,
And leave a legacy, forevermore.

12. Eternal Radiance: A Poem on the Many Forms of Beauty"

In ancient times, when Grecian gods still roamed the earth,

A concept was born, of unrivaled worth -

Beauty, the embodiment of all that is pure,

A treasure to cherish, forever to endure.

But as time passed, and civilizations rose,

Perceptions of beauty, like sand, did expose -

A fickleness, that with the winds does shift,

A subjectivity, that with the mind does rift.

For some, beauty is found in symmetry's grace,

A balance of form, in a pleasing embrace -

Others see beauty in that which is unique,

A rarity, that in its singularity speaks.

And yet, in the midst of this dichotomy,

A truth remains, immutable and free -

Beauty is but a reflection of the soul,

A radiance, that makes the heart whole.

For in the depths of the human spirit,

Lies a beauty, that none can inherit -

It is the beauty of love and compassion,

The beauty of selfless devotion.

But alas, mankind oft forgets this truth,

And in the superficial, finds solace uncouth -

Chasing after a beauty that fades with time,

Ignoring the beauty that lies within the mind.

And so, we are left with a world of illusion,

Where beauty is but a fleeting conclusion -

A fleeting thing, subject to change and decay,
A beauty that is never meant to stay.
But if we open our eyes and hearts once more,
We will find beauty that forever will soar -
A beauty that is not bound by shape or form,
A beauty that is always there, warm.
For beauty is not just in the eye of the beholder,
But in the depths of the human soldier -
It is the beauty of courage and of hope,
The beauty of the ability to cope.
In essence, beauty is but a state of mind,
A treasure that is always easy to find -
For beauty is not just in the things we see,
But in the way we choose to be.
But let us not forget that beauty also lies,
In the world that surrounds us and the skies -
Nature's canvas painted with hues divine,
A beauty that transcends space and time.
From the mountains that reach towards the sky,
To the oceans that ebb and flow nearby -
The beauty of the natural world is grand,
A sight that fills the heart and hand.
And as we take in this beauty around,
We are reminded of our own profound -
Connection to the earth and all that's alive,
A beauty that makes our souls thrive.
For beauty is not just for the chosen few,
But for all who choose to see it through -
It is a gift that is given to all,
A beauty that makes us feel tall.
But let us also remember this,

That beauty is not only in bliss -
It can also be found in hardship and pain,
For in growth, true beauty does gain.
So let us embrace beauty in all its forms,
From the tiniest flower to the mightiest storms -
For beauty is not just in things that we see,
But in the way we choose to be.
But let us also remember that beauty is fleeting,
A momentary sensation that is fleeting -
As the world around us shifts and changes,
Beauty transforms, and often rearranges.
And so, we must learn to see beyond,
The surface of things, and to the bond -
That connects us all, to something greater,
A beauty that is eternal and a true treasure.
For beauty is not just in what we can see,
But in the mystery, that surrounds us endlessly -
It is the beauty of the unknown,
A beauty that can never be shown.
And as we journey through life's winding path,
Let us seek out beauty, in every aftermath -
For it is the beauty that gives our lives meaning,
A beauty that is forever shining.
Thus, let us not be swayed by fleeting beauty,
But seek that which is truly our duty -
To find beauty in all its many forms,
And in our hearts, forever keep it warm.
Beauty is a multifaceted gem,
A treasure that is hard to comprehend -
It is found in the world and within the self,
A beauty that is both transient and eternal.

It is a concept that has been pondered for ages,

A subject that has inspired poets and sages -

For beauty is not just about what we see,

But about the way we choose to be.

So let us strive to see beauty in all things,

In the joy and in the sorrow it brings -

For in embracing beauty in all its forms,

Our hearts and souls are forever warmed.

Let us not be swayed by superficial charm,

But seek beauty in its truest form -

For it is the beauty that gives our lives grace,

A beauty that we can never replace.

And as we journey through life's winding way,

May beauty forever guide us on our way -

For it is the beauty that makes life worth living,

A beauty that is forever giving.

But let us also remember that beauty is not absolute,

It can be perceived differently by each and every brute -

It is a concept that is shaped by our experiences,

A beauty that is unique to each individual senses.

It is not something that can be quantified,

Or measured by any standards that are qualified -

For beauty is not something that can be rated,

It is something that is felt and appreciated.

And so, let us not try to define beauty,

For it is a concept that is constantly in motion and mutiny -

Let us instead, simply enjoy its presence,

And let it be the guiding light of our essence.

For in the end, beauty is not just a thing,

It is a feeling, a sensation, a state of being -

It is a reminder of the preciousness of life,

A beauty that brings joy and reduces strife.

But let us also remember that beauty is not just about physical appearance,

But also about the inner essence, the unseen, the endurance -

For true beauty is not just skin deep,

But a reflection of the person that one keeps.

It is the beauty of a kind heart,

And the beauty of a wise mind, that smart -

It is the beauty of compassion and empathy,

And the beauty of self-love and dignity.

For beauty is not just about physical attraction,

But also about inner connection, to self and to the action -

That brings us closer to our true selves,

And to the beauty that lies within, that excels.

And so, let us not be swayed by the superficial,

But seek beauty in its truest, most original -

For it is the beauty that lies within,

That truly makes us beautiful, and wins.

But let us also remember that beauty can be deceiving,

A façade that is not always worth believing -

For sometimes, the most beautiful things,

Are the ones that cause the most heartstrings.

Thus, let us not be fooled by outward appearances,

But strive to see the beauty in all things, even the most dense -

For true beauty is not just skin deep,

But a reflection of the person that one keeps.

And as we journey through life's winding roads,

Let us seek out the beauty that forever glows -

For it is the beauty that gives our lives meaning,

A beauty that is worth all the seeking.

But let us also remember that beauty is not everything,

For there are other things that life can bring -

Like love, and friendship, and happiness,

That make life worth living, and nothing less.

And as we embrace beauty in all its forms,

let us also recognize its transient norms -

For beauty is not meant to be forever captured,

But to be appreciated in the present, and cherished.

And as we appreciate beauty, let us also respect it,

For it is not something to be owned, or to be kept -

For beauty is not something to be possessed,

But to be shared, and to be blessed.

And as we share beauty, let us also protect it,

For it is something that is precious and delicate,

It is something that needs to be nurtured,

and not something that can be exploited or captured.

And as we embrace beauty, let us also remember,

That it is not just a thing, but an idea that we should treasure -

For beauty is not just something we see,

But something that we create, and something that we can be.

It is a state of mind, and a way of being,

A treasure that is always easy to find and freeing -

For beauty is not just in the things we see,

But in the way we choose to be.

So let us strive to be beautiful,

In our thoughts, in our actions and in our words so truthful -

For in doing so, we not only create beauty around us,

But also within us, a beauty that is forever and thus.

And as we create beauty, let us also share it,

For it is not something to be kept, but something to be spread and lit -

For in sharing beauty, we not only make the world a better place,

But also make our own lives, a true masterpiece.

And as we embrace beauty, let us also remember,

That it is not just a destination, but also a journey that we should endeavor -
For beauty is not just something to be attained,
But something to be constantly sought and maintained.
It is a process, a growth, and a discovery,
A treasure that is always worth the effort and inquiry -
For beauty is not just in the things we see,
But in the way we choose to be.
So let us strive to find beauty,
In every step of our journey, and every breath of our duty -
For in doing so, we not only discover beauty around us,
But also within us, a beauty that is forever and thus.
And as we discover beauty, let us also share it,
For it is not something to be kept, but something to be spread and lit -
For in sharing beauty, we not only make the world a better place,
But also make our own lives, a true masterpiece.
And as we embrace beauty, let us also remember,
That it is not just a thing, but a concept that is forever a member -
Of our existence, a part of our daily lives,
A treasure that is always there, and never hides.
It is a reminder, a guide, and a companion,
A treasure that is always worth the time and attention -
For beauty is not just in the things we see,
But in the way we choose to be.
So let us strive to find beauty,
In every moment of our lives, and every decision -
For in doing so, we not only discover beauty around us,
But also within us, a beauty that is forever and thus.
And as we discover beauty, let us also share it,
For it is not something to be kept, but something to be spread and lit -
For in sharing beauty, we not only make the world a better place,
But also make our own lives, a true masterpiece.

And as we embrace beauty, let us also remember,

That it is not just a thing, but a feeling that should never be a member -

Of our past, but a part of our present and future,

A treasure that is always there, and never a torture.

It is a hope, a dream, and a vision,

A treasure that is always worth the time and decision -

For beauty is not just in the things we see,

But in the way we choose to be.

So let us strive to find beauty,

In every step of our way, and every breath we take -

For in doing so, we not only discover beauty around us,

But also within us, a beauty that is forever and thus.

And as we discover beauty, let us also share it,

For it is not something to be kept, but something to be spread and lit -

For in sharing beauty, we not only make the world a better place,

But also make our own lives, a true masterpiece.

So let us embrace beauty, in all its forms,

And let it forever be the light that warms -

Our hearts, our minds, and our souls,

A beauty that makes life worth living, and whole.

13. The Pursuit of Knowledge: A Lifelong Journey of Understanding and Empowerment

In the halls of knowledge, where the learned dwell,

Lies the path to wisdom, a tale to tell.

Through the toil of study, and the strife of quest,

We learn to master ourselves, and our own behest.

For what is learning, but the gaining of insight,

Into the workings of the world, and the human plight?

Through the acquisition of facts, and the honing of skills,

We gain the power to shape our own wills.

But true learning goes beyond the mere accumulation of knowledge,

For it is the understanding of its application, that truly acknowledges.

For in the realm of learning, there is no end,

Only a constant quest, to comprehend.

So let us strive to learn, with eager mind and open heart,

For it is in the pursuit of knowledge, that true freedom starts.

And in the end, when our journey is through,

We shall look back with pride, at all that we knew.

For learning is not just an endeavor of the youth,

But a lifelong pursuit, a quest for truth.

It requires not just the exercise of the brain,

But the cultivation of the soul, and the cultivation of the heart.

For true learning brings about not just a broadened mind,

But a greater empathy, and a more compassionate kind.

It is the key to progress, and the path to growth,

For without learning, we are but stagnant, and lack forth.

It is the spark that ignites the fire of innovation,

And the compass that guides us to a brighter nation.

So let us embrace the power of learning,

And let it guide us to a brighter future, and a new yearning.

For in the pursuit of knowledge, lies the path to enlightenment,

And the key to unlocking the boundless potential of our being.

But let us not forget, that learning is not just about gaining information,

It's also about unlearning the biases and prejudices of our formation.

It's about challenging our assumptions, and questioning what we know,

It's about being open to new perspectives, and being receptive to the flow.

For true learning is not only about acquiring facts,

It's also about discovering what truly matters and what truly acts.

It's about understanding the connection between things,

And learning how to navigate through life, and how to spread our wings.

So let us strive to learn with an open mind,

And let us use that knowledge to be kind.

For learning is not just about achieving success,

It's about becoming the best version of ourselves, in all aspects.

And in the end, when our time here is through,

We'll look back with pride, knowing that we grew.

For learning is not just a solitary pursuit,

It's a collective endeavor, that requires us to be astute.

We learn from those around us, and those who came before,

We learn from our mistakes, and from the lessons of war.

We learn from the stories of the past, and the wisdom of the ages,

We learn from the diversity of cultures, and the different life stages.

Through collaboration, and through discourse,

We gain new insights, and new ways to endorse.

So let us strive to learn, not just for our own benefit,

But for the betterment of all, and the good of the merit.
For learning is not just about personal gain,
It's about leaving the world a better place, and breaking the chain.
For learning is not just about acquiring knowledge,
But also about understanding how to use it, and how to make it a leverage.
It's about understanding the connection between things,
And how to use that knowledge to make a change, and to make things sing.
It's about understanding the complexity of the world,
And how to navigate through it, and how to unfurl.
It's about understanding the human condition,
And how to work towards a better future, with compassion.
So let us strive to learn, with curiosity and vigor,
For it is the key to solving the world's problems, and the key to a bigger figure.
For in the pursuit of learning, lies the path to understanding,
And the key to creating a better world, and a brighter landing.
But let us not forget, that learning is not always easy,
It can be challenging, and it can make us queasy.
It requires effort, and dedication,
It requires us to be patient, and to have perspiration.
It can be frustrating, and it can be tiring,
But in the end, it's worth it, for the growth and the thriving.
For learning is not just about achieving success,
It's about becoming a better person, and to progress.
It's about gaining a deeper understanding,
And to make a positive impact, and to be demanding.
So let us embrace the challenge of learning,
And let us not be afraid, to be yearning.
For the pursuit of knowledge is a lifelong journey,
And the rewards are great, and the prize is plenty.
So let us strive to learn, with open hearts and open minds,
For it is in the pursuit of learning, that true fulfillment finds.

And let us not forget, that learning is not just about the head,

But also about the heart, and how it is fed.

It's not just about acquiring knowledge, but also about wisdom,

It's not just about understanding, but also about compassion.

For true learning requires us to be open and humble,

It requires us to be willing to admit when we fumble.

It's about understanding that we don't know everything,

And being open to new ideas, and being willing to sing.

So let us strive to learn, with humility and grace,

For it is in the pursuit of learning, that we find our place.

For learning is not just about achieving success,

But also about being a good person, and doing what is best.

And let us not forget that learning is not just about academics

It's also about life experiences and the lessons one can acquire in it.

It's about learning how to cope with adversity,

It's about learning how to build resilience and perseverance.

It's about learning how to be a good friend and a good partner,

It's about learning how to be a good listener, and a good advisor.

It's about learning how to be a good human being,

It's about learning how to be a good citizen and a good king.

So let us strive to learn from all aspects of life,

For it is through learning that we gain the insight and the drive.

For learning is not just about achieving success,

It's about becoming a better person, and making progress.

And let us not forget that learning is not just about the present,

But also about the future, and how we can prevent.

It's about understanding the consequences of our actions,

It's about understanding the impact we have on the environment, and the
satisfaction.

It's about learning how to create a sustainable world,

It's about learning how to be responsible and how to unfurl.

It's about learning how to create a better future for all,

It's about learning how to work together and how to stand tall.

So let us strive to learn, not just for ourselves,

But for the generations to come, and for the wealth.

And let us not forget that learning is not just about acquiring information,

It's also about how to critically evaluate it and how to question.

It's about learning how to think for oneself,

It's about learning how to form one's own opinions and how to be self-reliant.

It's about learning how to be a critical thinker,

It's about learning how to be a problem solver, and how to be a blinker.

It's about learning how to separate facts from fiction,

It's about learning how to discern truth from deception, and how to make a distinction.

So let us strive to learn, with a critical eye,

For it is through learning that we gain the ability to question and to try.

For learning is not just about achieving success,

It's about becoming a critical thinker and making progress.

And let us not forget that learning is not just about the acquisition of knowledge,

But also about the application of that knowledge and how it can be used to make a difference in the world.

It's about learning how to use our skills and talents to benefit others,

It's about learning how to be a force for good, and how to be a helper.

It's about learning how to make a positive impact on society,

It's about learning how to create change, and how to be a catalyst for unity.

So let us strive to learn, with a sense of purpose,

For it is through learning that we gain the ability to make a difference and to endorse.

For learning is not just about achieving success,

It's about making a positive impact on the world and making progress.

And let us not forget that learning is not just a one-time event,

But a continuous process, that requires commitment.

It's about learning to adapt to new situations and new information,

It's about learning to evolve and to take inspiration.

It's about learning to be flexible and open-minded,

It's about learning to be resilient and to be kind.

So let us strive to learn, with a sense of curiosity,

For it is through learning that we gain the ability to adapt and to flourish.

For learning is not just about achieving success,

It's about becoming a lifelong learner and making progress.

And let us not forget that learning is not just a one-time event,

But a continuous process, that requires commitment.

It's about learning to adapt to new situations and new information,

It's about learning to evolve and to take inspiration.

It's about learning to be flexible and open-minded,

It's about learning to be resilient and to be kind.

So let us strive to learn, with a sense of curiosity,

For it is through learning that we gain the ability to adapt and to flourish.

For learning is not just about achieving success,

It's about becoming a lifelong learner and making progress.

So let us embrace the power of learning,

For it is the path to personal growth, and a brighter yearning.

In the halls of knowledge, where the learned dwell,

Lies the path to wisdom, a tale to tell.

Let us be ever ready to learn, and ever willing to grow,

For in the pursuit of learning, lies the key to true enlightenment,

and the path to a brighter tomorrow.

14. The Mindful Journey: Finding Serenity in the Present."

In a world where chaos doth reign,

And thoughts of worry do oft pain,

A practice that doth bring serenity,

Is mindfulness, a mental tranquility.

With focus keen, and breath in sync,

One's mind and body in harmony link,

In the present moment, we do find,

A path to peace, that's truly kind.

For in the past, regrets doth linger,

And in the future, fears do in there,

But in the now, all is well,

And worries do dispel.

For mindfulness doth teach us this,

That all our worries are amiss,

For in the present, all is well,

And in that truth, we can excel.

So let us all strive to be,

Mindful in all that we do see,

For in that state of pure awareness,

Happiness and contentment is what we'll treasure.

It is a journey, not a destination,

A path to be walked with patience,

For mindfulness doth not come with ease,

It is a practice that requires diligence and keys.

The mind, a monkey that doth chatter,

With thoughts that scatter and flatter,

But mindfulness doth bring it to heel,
And in control, our mind doth feel.
It is a tool, to be wielded with care,
In the face of life's turmoil and snare,
For in the midst of chaos and strife,
Mindfulness brings meaning to life.
It doth not shield us from pain,
But it does grant us strength to sustain,
And in the face of adversity,
It grants us clarity and serenity.
So let us all strive to be,
Mindful in all that we do see,
For in that state of pure awareness,
We shall find true happiness and fairness.
For mindfulness doth show us the way,
To live in the moment, and not stray,
From the path of inner peace,
That brings release from the mind's increase.
It is a bridge to the heart,
Where love and compassion doth impart,
A connection to all that is real,
And the beauty of life we can feel.
It doth not seek to change the world,
But it can change the way we unfurl,
Our own thoughts and emotions,
And in that process, find solutions.
It doth not seek to escape,
But to face and to shape,
Our reality with understanding,
And in that process, find expanding.
For mindfulness doth open the door,

To a deeper sense of self and more,

It helps us to look within,

And discover the truth that lies therein.

It is a path to self-discovery,

And inner growth, without any hurry,

A journey of self-acceptance,

And finding true balance and relevance.

It doth not seek to be perfect,

But to accept and to connect,

With our own humanity,

And in that process, find humility.

It doth not seek to control,

But to let go and to roll,

With the changes of life,

And in that process, find inner light.

Mindfulness doth not seek to judge,

But to observe and to nudge,

The mind towards a peaceful state,

And in that process, find inner grace.

It is a journey of self-exploration,

And inner growth, with no hesitation,

A path to true understanding,

And finding peace in the present and expanding.

It doth not seek to be in control,

But to let go and to roll,

With the ebb and flow of life,

And in that process, find inner light.

It is a practice that doth transcend,

The boundaries of time and end,

It helps us to connect with the divine,

And in that process, find true alignment.

In a world where chaos doth prevail,
And troubles do oft assail,
Mindfulness doth bring repose,
And in that stillness, true clarity expose.
It is a practice that doth transcend,
The boundaries of time and end,
It helps us to connect with the divine,
And in that process, find true alignment.
It is a journey of self-discovery,
And inner growth, without any hurry,
A path to true understanding,
And finding peace in the present and expanding.
With mindfulness, we learn to see,
The beauty in simplicity,
And find contentment in the present,
Where true happiness and fulfillment is thus spent.
For mindfulness doth bring a new light,
To our perception, and make things right,
It helps us to see the world anew,
And in that process, true wisdom accrue.
It doth not seek to change the past,
But to learn from it, and make it last,
As a valuable lesson, that guides our way,
To a brighter future, come what may.
It is a journey of self-awareness,
And inner growth, without any pause,
A path to true understanding,
And finding peace in the present and expanding.
With mindfulness, we learn to let go,
Of our fears, doubts, and ego,
And find true freedom in the present,

Where true happiness and fulfillment is thus spent.
With mindfulness, we learn to embrace,
The beauty in life's fleeting pace,
And find contentment in the present,
Where true happiness and fulfillment is thus spent.
It is a practice that doth transcend,
The boundaries of time and end,
It helps us to connect with the divine,
And in that process, find true alignment.
For mindfulness doth bring a new sight,
To our perception, and make things right,
It helps us to see the world with new eyes,
And in that process, true wisdom arise.
It doth not seek to change the world,
But to change the way we unfurl,
Our own thoughts and emotions,
And in that process, find true devotion.
For mindfulness doth bring a new vision,
Of the world and our own decision,
It helps us to see things in a new way,
And in that process, true wisdom sway.
It doth not seek to change the past,
But to learn from it, and make it last,
As a valuable lesson, that guides our way,
To a brighter future, come what may.
It is a journey of self-discovery,
And inner growth, without any hurry,
A path to true understanding,
And finding peace in the present and expanding.
With mindfulness, we learn to see,
The beauty in simplicity,

And find contentment in the present,

Where true happiness and fulfillment is thus spent.

For mindfulness doth bring a new sense,

Of clarity and self- defense,

It helps us to navigate through life's storms,

And in that process, true wisdom adorns.

It doth not seek to change the future,

But to live in the present, and be a suture,

That mends the past and the future,

To make a present that is truly pure.

It is a journey of self-acceptance,

And inner growth, with no reluctance,

A path to true understanding,

And finding peace in the present and expanding.

With mindfulness, we learn to let go,

Of our fears, doubts, and ego,

And find true freedom in the present,

Where true happiness and fulfillment is thus spent.

So let us all strive to be,

Mindful in all that we do see,

For in that state of pure awareness,

We shall find true liberation and largess.

Thank You

Khublei shi hajar nguh.

Note

As I, a breviloquent raptor, wield A lever, with naught else to my design, I generate tones for the aural field In this prosaic orb we call mankind. My actions, though, are but a small part Of forces far beyond my control, For nature holds the key to each chart And sets the laws that govern the whole. But still, I am compelled to explore The workings of this vast machinery, To seek the truth that lies at core And find the answers to humanity. Though some may call it quest I'll seek the truth, with no time to rest.

www.ingramcontent.com/pod-product-compliance
Lightning Source LLC
Chambersburg PA
CBHW020734160726
47993CB00006B/2453